# LET'S PARTY AT MULATE'S

# LET'S PARTY AT MULATE'S

By Monique Boutté Christina

Foreword by
Renée Grace Christina

PELICAN PUBLISHING COMPANY
Gretna 2019

Copyright © 2019
By Monique Boutté Christina
All rights reserved

*The word "Pelican" and the depiction of a pelican are trademarks of Pelican Publishing Company, Inc., and are registered in the U.S. Patent and Trademark Office.*

Library of Congress Cataloging-in-Publication Data

Names: Christina, Monique Boutte, author. | Mulate's (Restaurant : New Orleans, La.)
Title: Let's party at Mulate's / by Monique Boutte Christina ; foreword by Renee Grace Christina.
Description: Gretna, Louisiana : Pelican Publishing Company, Inc., [2019] | Includes indexes.
Identifiers: LCCN 2019007386| ISBN 9781455624577 (pbk. : alk. paper) | ISBN 9781455624584 (ebook)
Subjects: LCSH: Cooking, American--Louisiana style. | Cooking, Cajun.
Classification: LCC TX715.2.L68 C47 2019 | DDC 641.59763--dc23 LC record available at https://lccn.loc.gov/2019007386

Printed in the United States of America

Published by Pelican Publishing Company, Inc.
1000 Burmaster Street, Gretna, Louisiana 70053
www.pelicanpub.com

*FOR MY DAD, KERRY BOUTTÉ, ONE OF THE VISIONARIES WHO BROUGHT CAJUN CULTURE TO THE WORLD.*

Kerry and Monique.

# CONTENTS

Foreword **9**
Acknowledgments **13**
Introduction **15**

### FAVORITE RECIPES

Soups & Salads **19**
Seafood **29**
Meat & Poultry **49**
Vegetables & Sides **61**
Sweets **69**

### ENTERTAINING

Party Planning Guide **77**
Brunch **83**
Crawfish Boil **91**
Sunday Lunch **99**
Game Day Party **107**
Dinner Party **113**
Sunday Barbecue **121**
Thanksgiving Day **129**
Christmas Eve **139**
Christmas Morning **145**
New Year's Day **151**

Indexes **158**

Founder Kerry Boutté and his granddaughter Renée.

# FOREWORD

My family's restaurant, Mulate's, is known as "The Original Cajun Restaurant." The vision of my grandfather Kerry Boutté, it is famous for keeping old traditions alive with everything from Cajun music and dancing to authentic Cajun food. Mulate's is a place where Cajuns come to celebrate their heritage, and the world comes to join them.

Cajun music has had a major influence on the culture in Louisiana. This form of music, traditionally sung in French, was brought down to southwest Louisiana by Acadian settlers from Nova Scotia. Music was the center of social gatherings for early Cajuns and was commonly played in people's homes and during Sunday afternoon fais do-dos. The term fais do-do refers to adults putting their children to sleep, or going "do-do," so the parents could return to the fun. In recent times, this term has come to refer to public events where people gather and dance to music.

The earliest instrument associated with Cajun music is the fiddle. In a method commonly referred to as "twin fiddling," one fiddle plays the melody while the other plays the harmony. Over time, new instruments have been brought into the mix, with the accordion being the most vital and the most famous over the course of the twentieth century. The accordion has attracted fans for three important reasons: it has a powerful, rhythmic sound, it is almost indestructible, and basic proficiency can be developed fairly easily.

While he was growing up, Kerry Boutté's parents never played Cajun music, and his friends rarely attended clubs that played Cajun music. At his graduation party, which happened to be held at a Cajun nightclub, he got his first taste of the music and grew to love it. In 1968, Kerry Boutté joined the army and was stationed in Germany. There he developed an interest in art, which is reflected in the art that today covers the walls of Mulate's. It was also in Germany that he discovered beer gardens: extravagant, fun places where people gather to eat, drink, and listen to German music. He saw a connection with his own culture. He came back to Louisiana with a great desire to bring this experience to the people of his home state and incorporate the local Cajun food and culture. What better way than to open his own restaurant with live music?

In 1980, Kerry Boutté opened Mulate's in a small building in Breaux Bridge, Louisiana. On their first day, he and his four employees served two customers. Despite the small turnout, Boutté was determined to bring live music into his seafood restaurant. As he inquired about musicians, accordion player

Pat Breaux gave him a name. That name was Zachary Richard, and he was the first musician to perform at Mulate's. Only ten people came to Mulate's the night he performed, but with Richard's performance, Boutté was the first to combine food with music to create the Cajun supper club atmosphere for which Mulate's is now famous.

Four years later, Boutté got his first opportunity to share the Mulate's experience with the world. The World's Fair came to New Orleans, and he booked buses to bring World's Fair visitors from New Orleans to his restaurant in Breaux Bridge. As the restaurant grew in popularity and fame, Boutté opened a Baton Rouge location in 1988 then a New Orleans location in 1990.

Since then, Mulate's has become a family affair. Boutté's daughter Monique started working at the Baton Rouge location in 1991 as a hostess and cashier while attending Louisiana State University. In 1997, when the location in New Orleans proved to be a challenge for Boutté to run by himself, he asked Monique to drop everything and come to New Orleans to help him correct the finances and restore the business. When Monique wanted to step away to have children, her husband, Murphy, a lawyer by trade, joined the business in 2000. Both the Breaux Bridge and Baton Rouge locations have since closed, so together Monique and Murphy concentrate all their time and effort on the New Orleans restaurant.

When Hurricane Katrina hit in 2005, Mulate's had to temporarily close due to the devastating damage to the building and the city. Although Mulate's is in the sliver of the city that did not flood, it suffered extensive damage as a result of its proximity to the survivor camp at the Convention Center. Luckily, the team was able to reopen a smaller dining room in their private event space just four months later. The entire restaurant reopened in April 2006. Mulate's suffered another setback when it lost a portion of its roof to a hurricane in 2012, but again the restaurant was rebuilt.

Today, anyone who walks in the restaurant is greeted by the Cajun vibe Boutté so thoughtfully created. People flock to the restaurant for the live Cajun music that is performed every night. From children to senior citizens, everyone has a great time in the inviting family atmosphere.

I have been blessed to have this restaurant in my life. I love learning about the culture I was born into. Even though Mulate's has gone through many ups and downs, it has continued to live up to its title as "The Original Cajun Restaurant."

*Renée Grace Christina*

Kerry and his wife, Tiffa.

My family, complete with three Frenchies: Remi, Sadie, and Beaudie.

# ACKNOWLEDGMENTS

I am truly blessed with amazing people in my life. A special thank you to . . .

My beautiful family, Murphy, Renée, and Maia.
They were all great recipe tasters, and each helped me in their own way.

My mom and dad for all their support throughout my entire life.

Leether, Tiffa, Ida, Joyce, Mary Grace, and Ms. G for being strong women who continue to inspire my life and cooking. As Ms. G would say, "Don't sweat the small stuff."

Kelly Diket for helping to shop, prep, taste, and clean up the kitchen.
You keep me together when my mind is in a thousand places.
Our family is truly blessed to have you in our lives.

Chantelle Washington, our director of sales,
for always being by my side for the last twenty-plus years.

Perry Watts for being an amazing chef and the
hardest-working employee in the building.

Tamie Johnson and the management team of Jairo Jaramillo,
Timothy Morris, Callie Sloan, and Michael Williams for making it happen every day.
Your loyalty is the foundation of the restaurant.

Tressie Kidder for helping me design the cover of the book,
which proved to be a more difficult task than I thought!

George Kuchler of GK Photography for his patience and
the amazing shots he's taken at Mulate's and in my home.

Kristi Kosloski for her help with ideas and editing the book.

Ethan Branch and Spencer Lanosga for being awesome
recipe tasters who make me so happy when they enjoy my food.

My network of beautiful girlfriends, mostly from my neighborhood. Without
their support and willingness to be photographed, I couldn't have done this.

Monique and Murphy in the Teche Room at Mulate's.

# INTRODUCTION

I wrote the first Mulate's cookbook in 2006, so it was definitely time to write a second one. *Recipes from Mulate's* came out just a few months after Hurricane Katrina, which seems like a lifetime ago. It contained restaurant and family recipes. In raising my two daughters, I discovered how important it is to me to share recipes from generation to generation. This book contains some of the same recipes from my first cookbook because they are so good that they simply must be included, but this book focuses on party planning and entertaining since that is what Mulate's does best.

The first part of this book is set up like a traditional cookbook and it contains some of the family's favorite recipes. The second part is the party planning section, complete with menus, many of which we offer in our private rooms. Mulate's has two private event spaces, the Teche Room and the cozier Acadia Room. In total, we have more than 10,000 square feet of entertaining space. Since many people love a signature drink, I have also included suggested drink options for each event. Feel free to change up the menus as you see fit, using the recipes from the earlier chapters in the book.

In Louisiana, we love to throw a good party, so let's party! As we say in south Louisiana, *"Laissez les bon temps rouler!"*

# FAVORITE RECIPES

Included in this section are family recipes, both old and new,
as well as recipes for some of the delicious items we serve at Mulate's.
Hopefully, these recipes will become your family favorites as well!

Dancing the two-step.

# SOUPS & SALADS

# Crawfish Bisque

*Although time consuming and utilizing lots of ingredients, this classic bisque is always a favorite in my house. Traditionally, you stuff the crawfish heads with the stuffing mixture, but I prefer to make boulettes to drop in the bisque.*

### BOULETTES

1 stick unsalted butter
1½ cups diced onions
½ cup diced bell pepper
1 stalk celery, diced
2 cloves garlic, minced
2 tsp. Mulate's Cajun Seasoning
1 tsp. kosher salt
½ tsp. cayenne pepper
¾ cup chicken stock
40 crawfish tails, chopped
1 tbsp. crawfish fat
¾ cup breadcrumbs
1 egg, whisked
¼ cup finely sliced green onions
Flour to roll boulettes

### BISQUE

1 stick unsalted butter
½ cup flour
2 cups diced onions
½ cup diced bell pepper
½ cup diced celery
3 cloves garlic, minced
40 crawfish tails, whole
1 tbsp. crawfish fat
2 tsp. Mulate's Cajun Seasoning
2 tsp. kosher salt
3 cups chicken or vegetable stock
½ cup finely sliced green onions, for garnish
½ cup finely chopped flat leaf parsley, for garnish

Preheat oven to 350 degrees. Line a baking sheet with non-stick aluminum foil. In a large skillet, melt butter over medium heat. Cook onion, bell pepper, and celery for 15 minutes until softened and lightly brown. Add garlic and dry seasonings and cook for 3 minutes more. Stir in chicken stock, crawfish tails, and crawfish fat and cook for 5 minutes. Remove from heat. Allow mixture to cool for 15 minutes then transfer to a mixing bowl. Add breadcrumbs, egg, and green onion and stir to combine. Form mixture into 3 oz. balls. Roll in flour and bake for 35 minutes. Set aside while you prepare the Bisque.

In a large skillet, over medium-low heat, melt butter and add flour. Stir continuously for 8-10 minutes to make a roux the color of peanut butter. Fold in onion, bell pepper, and celery and cook for 5 minutes. Add garlic and cook for 3 minutes more. Add crawfish tails, fat, and dry seasonings and cook for 3 minutes. Stir in stock and simmer for about 20 minutes.

Spoon bisque into a bowl and add 3-4 crawfish boulettes. Garnish with green onions and parsley. Serves 6-8.

# Chicken & Sausage Gumbo

*Every Cajun puts a pot of gumbo on the stove when the first cold snap of the fall comes through. And by "cold snap," I mean when the temperature drops below 70 degrees!*

3 lb. chicken, cut into pieces

Mulate's Cajun Seasoning, to taste

1 tbsp. vegetable oil

2 cups diced onions

1 cup diced bell pepper

1 tbsp. salt

1 tsp. cayenne pepper

4 qt. water

1 cup dark roux

3 links smoked sausage, cut into ½-inch rounds

Cooked white rice

Season all chicken pieces with Mulate's Cajun Seasoning. In a large soup pot, heat oil over medium-high heat. Working in batches so as not to overcrowd the pot, brown the chicken on both sides. Remove and set aside. Add onion and bell pepper to the pot and cook for about 5 minutes. Add dry seasonings to the vegetables, then add water and bring to a boil. Add roux, stirring constantly until smooth. Add chicken back to the pot and simmer over medium heat for 1 hour. Add smoked sausage and cook for 20 minutes more. Serve over white rice. Serves 6-8.

---

**Note:** You can buy a dark roux (which will save time) in most grocery stores, but you can make your own as well. To make a roux for this recipe, heat 1 cup vegetable oil in a heavy pot or pan. Add 1 cup all-purpose flour and cook over a low heat, stirring constantly until the roux is the color you desire. For this gumbo, the roux should be a chocolate brown color. Making your own roux requires time and patience. You can't rush it!

# Roasted Corn & Shrimp Bisque

*We serve this creamy bisque in the restaurant during the fall and winter. Although most of our customers want to sample our gumbo, this is a delicious alternative.*

1 stick unsalted butter
2 cups diced onions
3 cloves garlic, minced
½ cup flour
1 tbsp. Mulate's Cajun Seasoning
1½ tsp. kosher salt
1 tsp. garlic powder
8 cups whole milk
2 cups half-and-half
1 can whole kernel corn
1 can cream-style corn
1½ lb. 40/50 count shrimp, peeled and deveined

In a large soup pot, melt butter over medium heat. Add onions and cook for 5-8 minutes. Add garlic and continue cooking for 3 minutes. Stir frequently to make sure that garlic doesn't brown. Add flour a little at a time, stirring constantly for 5 minutes until a blonde (light) roux forms. Add dry seasonings and continue stirring. Gradually add milk and half-and-half, stirring constantly until well blended. Increase heat to medium-high. Bring just to a boil then reduce heat to medium-low.

Meanwhile, drain the can of whole kernel corn. In a medium skillet, heat corn over medium-high heat and toss to lightly roast. Add roasted whole kernel corn and can of cream-style corn to soup; mix well. Add shrimp and partially cover. Continue cooking, stirring frequently, until soup is desired thickness, about 15 minutes. Taste soup and season if necessary. Serves 8 as an appetizer.

# Cajun Cobb Salad

*A Cajun spin on a classic salad. The spicy, salty andouille is much heartier than the usual choice of bacon for this salad.*

## CAJUN COBB SALAD

1 cup Andouille sausage, thinly sliced into triangles

1 lb. 21/25 count shrimp, peeled and deveined

1 tbsp. Mulate's Cajun Seasoning

1 tbsp. extra virgin olive oil

4 cups romaine or butter lettuce, sliced

20 grape tomatoes, sliced in half

2 avocados, chunked

4 boiled eggs, sliced into wedges

1 can fried onions

Spicy Blue Cheese Dressing

In a large skillet, over medium heat, cook andouille for 8-10 minutes to brown. Remove from skillet and set aside. Season shrimp with Mulate's Cajun Seasoning. Heat olive oil in the skillet then add shrimp. Cook shrimp for 3 minutes on each side, or until pink and cooked through. Remove from skillet and set aside.

Place lettuce in a large serving bowl. On top of the lettuce, arrange the tomatoes in a row down the middle of the bowl. In rows on either side of the tomatoes, place the avocado, shrimp, egg, and andouille. Top with crispy fried onions. Serve with Spicy Blue Cheese dressing on the side. Serves 4-6.

## SPICY BLUE CHEESE DRESSING

$\frac{1}{3}$ cup mayonnaise

$\frac{1}{3}$ cup sour cream

1 tbsp. fresh lemon juice

Pinch salt

10 turns of fresh cracked pepper

2 tsp. Mulate's Cayenne Pepper Sauce

$\frac{2}{3}$ cup blue cheese crumbles

In a bowl, combine all ingredients except blue cheese. Mix thoroughly then fold in blue cheese.

---

*Note:* Mulate's products can be found online at www.mulates.com and are available for purchase from the restaurant.

# Shrimp Remoulade

*Served as a dipping sauce with grilled or fried alligator, Mulate's Remoulade is our house dressing. Although we make all of our dressings from scratch, this is a customer favorite. You can add shrimp, crabmeat, or crawfish to the dressing and serve as a salad on top of chopped lettuce.*

### SHRIMP REMOULADE

2 lb. 40/50 count shrimp, boiled in salted water (or crab boil if you like them spicy!)
Remoulade Dressing
Sliced green onions, for garnish
1 head lettuce, chopped

Top shrimp with Remoulade Dressing and garnish with green onion. Serve over lettuce. Serves 10.

### REMOULADE DRESSING

2 cups mayonnaise
½ cup + 1 tbsp. Creole mustard
2 tsp. Worcestershire sauce
6 dashes Mulate's Cayenne Pepper sauce
½ tsp. paprika

Combine all ingredients. Refrigerate until ready to serve.

# Fried Oyster Caesar Salad

*You won't find a better Caesar dressing recipe than this one! For those who love oysters, this is a fantastic combination.*

**CAESAR SALAD**
2 small garlic cloves, minced
1 tsp. anchovy paste
2 tbsp. fresh lemon juice
1 tsp. Worcestershire sauce
1 tsp. Dijon mustard
1 cup mayonnaise
¼ tsp. kosher salt
¼ tsp. fresh cracked black pepper
½ cup Parmesan cheese
2 heads romaine lettuce, rinsed and chopped

To make the dressing, combine all ingredients except lettuce. Toss lettuce with dressing and top with Fried Oysters. Arrange 6 oysters around the edge of each plate. Serves 4-6.

**FRIED OYSTERS**
3 cups cornmeal
1 tbsp. Mulate's Cajun Seasoning
1 tsp. salt
24-36 fresh oysters
2 cups cottonseed oil

In a large skillet, heat oil to 375 degrees. Place cornmeal in a 9x13 pan. Add seasonings to the cornmeal; mix well. Place oysters, 8-10 at a time, in the seasoned cornmeal and coat well. Working in batches, fry oysters for 2-3 minutes per side, depending on desired crispiness. Drain cooked oysters on a plate lined with paper towels.

Murphy jamming on the washboard with Lee Benoit.

# SEAFOOD

# Catfish Jambalaya

*Back in 1980, when my dad opened Mulate's in Breaux Bridge, Louisiana, this was the jambalaya he served. I can still remember watching him make it fresh every morning. We changed the dish to chicken and sausage jambalaya when we opened Mulate's in New Orleans because those flavors appealed to a wider audience. These flavors bring me right back to the old days.*

1½ sticks unsalted butter
1½ cups diced onions
½ cup diced bell pepper
¼ cup diced celery
1½ cups chopped mushrooms
10 oz. can Ro-Tel diced tomatoes
3 cloves garlic, minced
1½ tsp. salt
½ tsp. black pepper
¼ tsp. cayenne pepper
2-3 cups cooked rice
3 small catfish fillets, lightly seasoned with salt and cayenne pepper

In a large pot, melt butter over medium heat. Add onion, bell pepper, and celery. Cook for 30 minutes, stirring frequently, until vegetables are very tender and slightly brown. Mix in mushrooms, diced tomatoes, garlic, salt, black pepper, and cayenne pepper, and cook for 10 minutes. Remove from heat and mix in cooked rice to desired consistency.

Meanwhile, in a large skillet over medium heat, sauté catfish for 3-4 minutes per side or until fully cooked. Fold cooked catfish into rice so as not to break the catfish up completely. Serves 6-8.

# Catfish Mulate's

*Our house specialty.*

Our house specialty, Catfish Mulate's, served with jambalaya and a stuffed potato.

¼ cup vegetable oil
4 catfish fillets (7-9 oz. each)
1 tsp. kosher salt
1 tsp. cayenne pepper
Flour for dusting fillets

Heat oil in a large pan over medium-high heat. Season catfish fillets with salt and cayenne pepper. Lightly dust one side of the fillet with flour. Place fish in pan flour side down. Cook catfish for 7 minutes, then turn and cook 5 minutes more. Transfer catfish to a serving plate and top with Crawfish Étouffée (see Index). Serves 4.

# Crab Cakes with Spicy Cajun Aioli

*Jumbo lump crabmeat, minimal fillers... You can't go wrong!*

**CRAB CAKES**

2 eggs, whisked
⅓ cup mayonnaise
1 tsp. Dijon mustard
2 tsp. Mulate's Cajun Seasoning
½ tsp. garlic powder
2 tbsp. finely sliced green onion
1 tbsp. finely chopped parsley
1 tbsp. finely diced red bell pepper
½ cup Parmesan cheese, divided
1⅔ cup panko breadcrumbs, divided
1 lb. jumbo lump crabmeat
2 tbsp. extra virgin olive oil

**SPICY CAJUN AIOLI**

¾ cup mayonnaise
1 tbsp. spicy brown mustard
1 tbsp. ketchup
1 tsp. Mulate's Cayenne Pepper Sauce
¼ tsp. cayenne pepper
1 tbsp. fresh chopped parsley

Combine all ingredients, mix well, and serve. Makes about 1 cup.

In a large mixing bowl, combine eggs, mayonnaise, and mustard. Stir in Mulate's Cajun Seasoning and garlic powder. Add green onion, parsley, red bell pepper, ¼ cup Parmesan cheese, and ⅔ cup breadcrumbs; mix. Gently fold in jumbo lump crabmeat. Using a 3-inch ring-form, tightly pack crabmeat mixture into cakes and arrange on a sheet pan. Refrigerate at least 1 hour so crab cakes will hold together during cooking.

Preheat oven to 350 degrees. Combine remaining Parmesan cheese and breadcrumbs in an 8x8 baking dish. Dredge cakes in breadcrumb mixture, coating each side. Heat the oil in a large skillet over medium-high heat. Brown the crab cakes on both sides then place on a sheet pan. Bake for 5-10 minutes. Serve with Spicy Cajun Aioli. Makes 6-8 crab cakes.

# Mulate's Crabmeat Stuffing

*We still follow the recipe my dad used when he founded Mulate's in Breaux Bridge, Louisiana! My favorite way to eat this stuffing is in our Stuffed Mushroom appetizer.*

**MULATE'S CRABMEAT STUFFING**

2 sticks unsalted butter
4 cups diced onions
2 cups diced bell pepper
½ cup diced celery
2 cloves garlic, minced
1 tbsp. Mulate's Cajun Seasoning
12 hamburger buns
½ cup sliced green onions
2 tbsp. fresh chopped parsley
3 eggs, whisked
1 lb. claw crabmeat

Melt butter in a large pot over medium-low heat. Add onions, bell pepper, celery, and garlic. Cook until tender and caramelized, about 45 minutes. Add Mulate's Cajun Seasoning and mix well. Set aside.

For these next steps, it's best to use your hands. In a large bowl, crumble hamburger buns. Add green onions and parsley; toss well. Mix in eggs. Add cooked vegetables; mix well. Fold in crabmeat. Makes approximately 2 lb. of stuffing.

**STUFFED MUSHROOMS**

30 medium white mushroom caps
2 eggs, whisked
1 cup milk
3 cups breadcrumbs
2-3 cups cottonseed oil

Stuff the mushroom caps with Mulate's Crabmeat Stuffing and set aside. In a shallow bowl or plate, combine eggs and milk. Place the breadcrumbs on a separate plate. Dip the stuffed mushrooms in the egg wash then coat in breadcrumbs. Fry in oil at 350 degrees until golden brown. Serves 6-8 as an appetizer.

# Crabmeat au Gratin

*For this decadent dish, I like to use 1 lb. of jumbo lump crabmeat and 1 lb. of claw crabmeat. I love the flavor of the claw meat, and its use reduces the expense of the dish since jumbo lump crabmeat can be extremely pricey at certain times of the year.*

- 1 stick unsalted butter
- 1 cup diced onions
- 2 tsp. kosher salt
- 1 tsp. cayenne pepper
- 5 tbsp. flour
- 2 cups half-and-half
- 1½ cups whole milk
- 2 cups Cheddar cheese, divided
- 2 egg yolks, combined
- 2 lb. crabmeat

Preheat oven to 400 degrees. In a medium saucepot, melt butter over medium heat. Add onion and cook for 10 minutes, or until onion is translucent. Add salt, cayenne pepper, and flour, stirring constantly to combine. Stir in half-and-half and milk then bring to a boil. Stir in 1 cup of cheese. When the cheese has melted, remove from heat. Add egg yolks; mix well. Fold in crabmeat. Transfer to buttered au gratin dishes. Top each with cheese. Bake for about 15 minutes, or until cheese is melted and bubbly. Makes 8 au gratins.

# Mulate's Special Soft-Shell Crab

*When fresh soft-shell crabs are in season, we always pick up a few dozen to serve as a special in the restaurant. My husband loves them fried, and the cream sauce adds depth to the dish.*

### MULATE'S SPECIAL SOFT-SHELL CRAB

4 fresh soft-shell crabs, cleaned
Vegetable oil
1 egg
½ cup milk
1 cup all-purpose flour
1 tbsp. Mulate's Cajun Seasoning
1 tsp. salt
3-4 cups cottonseed oil

To clean the crab, lift one side of the top shell and remove the gills. Put top shell back in place and repeat process on the other side. Remove the tail flap on the underside of the crab. Using a pair of scissors, remove the face by cutting behind the eyes. Rinse the crabs thoroughly with cold water. Set aside to dry on paper towels.

Pour oil into a deep fryer and heat to 375 degrees. In a shallow dish, whisk together the egg and milk. In a separate bowl, season flour with Mulate's Cajun Seasoning and salt. Dip each crab in the egg mixture, then dredge in flour, shaking off excess. Holding the crab by the claws, carefully lower crab into the deep fryer. Cook for 2 minutes, or until golden brown on one side. Carefully turn the crab and cook until golden on both sides. Drain on paper towels. Top with Crawfish Cream Sauce and serve as soon as crabs are cool enough to eat. Serves 4.

### CRAWFISH CREAM SAUCE

½ cup unsalted butter
½ cup all-purpose flour
1 cup heavy cream
2 tsp. Mulate's Cajun Seasoning
½ tsp. salt, optional
½ lb. crawfish tails

In a sauce pan, melt butter over medium heat. Stir in flour and cook for 5 minutes. Add heavy cream, stirring constantly until it incorporates. Add Mulate's Cajun Seasoning and salt and continue cooking for 5 more minutes. Add crawfish and cook an additional 5 minutes. Serve over soft-shell crab.

# Crawfish Bread

*My version of the festival favorite!*

- 4 tbsp. unsalted butter
- 1 lb. crawfish tails
- 2 cloves garlic, minced
- 1 tbsp. Mulate's Cajun Seasoning
- ½ tsp. cayenne pepper
- ¼ cup sliced green onions
- ¾ cup shredded Monterey Jack cheese
- ¼ cup Parmesan cheese
- ½ cup mayonnaise
- 1 loaf of French bread (12-inches), cut in half

Preheat oven to 350 degrees. In a large skillet, melt butter over medium heat. Add crawfish tails, garlic, Mulate's Cajun Seasoning, and cayenne pepper. Let this mixture cook for 8 minutes. Remove from heat and mix in green onions. Set aside to cool for 10 minutes.

Meanwhile, in a bowl, fold the mayonnaise into the cheeses. Add cooled crawfish mixture to the cheese mixture and toss to combine.

Cut the French bread halves lengthwise. Spoon the mixture onto the bread. Bake for 15 minutes, or until cheese is melted. Broil for an additional 2-3 minutes, watching closely so that the bread does not burn. Remove bread from oven and allow it to cool before cutting the bread into serving size portions. Serves 8-10.

# Crawfish Étouffée

*You can't go wrong with this traditional favorite! Best made during crawfish season with fresh crawfish tails, it is still delicious if you have to make it out of season.*

4 tbsp. unsalted butter
¼ cup flour
1 cup diced onions
2 cloves garlic, minced
3 cups vegetable or chicken stock
1 bay leaf
1 tbsp. Mulate's Cajun Seasoning
1 lb. crawfish tails with fat
Cooked rice

In a large skillet, melt butter over medium-low heat. Add flour, stirring constantly for 8-10 minutes to make a roux the color of peanut butter. Add onion and cook for 5 minutes, or until onion is tender. Add garlic and cook for 3 minutes more. Mix in stock, bay leaf, and Mulate's Cajun Seasoning; simmer for 20 minutes. Add crawfish and any collected crawfish fat. If you are using packaged crawfish, add 1 tbsp. water to the bag and swish it around. Pour the water into the pot so you don't miss any good flavor! Simmer for 5-10 minutes. Remove bay leaf. Serve over rice. Serves 4-6.

# Crawfish Fettuccine

*Cheesy and delicious. Need I say more?*

2 sticks unsalted butter, divided
1 cup diced onions
½ cup diced bell pepper
2 10 oz. cans cream of mushroom soup
2 lbs. crawfish tails with fat
½ tsp. cayenne pepper
½ tsp. black pepper
1 pt. half-and-half, divided
1 tsp. flour
1 lb. processed cheese, cubed
1 lb. cooked fettuccine

In a large saucepot, melt 1 stick of butter over medium heat. Sauté onion and bell pepper for 8-10 minutes, or until onion is transparent. Stir in cream of mushroom soup. Cook for 10 minutes. Add crawfish, cayenne pepper, and black pepper and cook for another 10 minutes. Add half-and-half as needed to prevent sticking.

In a separate saucepan, melt remaining stick of butter over medium-low heat. Add flour, stirring constantly for 5 minutes. Add 1 cup half-and-half and increase heat to medium. Cook an additional 5 minutes. Add cheese to pot, stirring until cheese is melted. Add half-and-half as needed to keep sauce from becoming too thick.

Add cheese sauce to crawfish-mushroom sauce. Stir to combine well. Add cooked fettuccine and toss to coat. Serves 8.

# Crawfish Pie

*A special crawfish treat with no fillers!*

4 tbsp. unsalted butter
1 cup diced onions
½ cup diced bell pepper
¼ cup diced celery
2 cloves garlic, minced
1 tsp. kosher salt
¼ tsp. cayenne pepper
1 lb. crawfish tails
3 tbsp. cornstarch
½ cup water
2 tbsp. sliced green onions
1 tbsp. fresh chopped parsley
1 9-inch pie crust

Preheat oven to 375 degrees. In a large skillet, melt butter over medium heat. Sauté onions, bell pepper, and celery in butter until lightly browned and softened. Mix in garlic, salt, cayenne pepper, and crawfish. Cook for 5 minutes.

If you are using packaged crawfish, pour ½ cup water into the empty crawfish bag and swish it around to catch all that extra flavor. Pour the water into a small bowl and whisk in the cornstarch until smooth. Stir the cornstarch mixture into the crawfish and simmer for 5 minutes, or until mixture begins to thicken. Remove from heat and add green onions and parsley.

Pour crawfish mixture into pie crust and bake for 35-40 minutes. Let stand for 5-10 minutes before serving. Serves 6-8.

## Blackened Shrimp au Gratin

*This spicy au gratin comes on our Shrimp Quartet. It's a simple way to change up the old favorite!*

2 lb. 40/50 count shrimp, peeled and deveined
1-2 tbsp. Cajun blackening seasoning
1 stick + 4 tbsp. unsalted butter, divided
1 cup diced onions
2 tsp. kosher salt
1 tsp. cayenne pepper
5 tbsp. flour
2 cups half-and-half
1½ cups whole milk
2 cups Cheddar cheese, divided
2 egg yolks, whisked

Season the shrimp with blackening seasoning. In a large skillet, heat 4 tbsp. butter and cook shrimp for 6-8 minutes, until pink and cooked through. Set aside.

Preheat oven to 400 degrees. In a medium saucepot, melt 1 stick butter over medium heat. Sauté onion in butter for 5-8 minutes, or until softened. Add salt, cayenne pepper, and flour. Stirring constantly, slowly add half-and-half and milk; bring to a low boil. Stir in 1 cup Cheddar cheese. When the cheese has melted, remove from heat and let cool for 5 minutes. Add egg yolks; mix well.

Coat the bottom of a buttered au gratin dish with sauce. Layer shrimp then top with more sauce. Top with cheese. Bake for about 15 minutes, or until cheese is melted and bubbly. Makes 8 au gratins.

## Smothered Okra with Shrimp

*I love, love, love okra. This is a simple way to have it as a complete meal.*

1 tbsp. vegetable oil
¾ cup diced onions
1 tbsp. Mulate's Cajun Seasoning
1 tsp. kosher salt
2 lb. cut okra
10 oz. can Ro-Tel diced tomatoes
1 cup reduced sodium chicken broth
1 lb. 21/25 count shrimp, peeled and deveined
Cooked white rice, optional

In a large pot, heat oil over medium heat. Sauté onions for 5-10 minutes, or until softened. Mix in Mulate's Cajun Seasoning, salt, okra, tomatoes, and broth. Bring to a simmer then reduce heat to low. Simmer, covered, for 45 minutes, stirring occasionally. If the okra begins to stick, add water a little at a time and scrape the bottom of the pot. Add the shrimp and cook for 5-8 minutes, or until shrimp are pink. Serve as is or over white rice. Serves 6-8.

# Shrimp Étouffée

*I like to make this when I'm craving étouffée but crawfish are out of season.*

4 tbsp. unsalted butter
¼ cup flour
1 cup diced onions
¼ cup diced bell pepper
2 cloves garlic, minced
3 cups vegetable or chicken broth
1 tbsp. Mulate's Cajun Seasoning
1 tsp. kosher salt
1 tsp. garlic powder
1 bay leaf
1 lb. 40/50 count shrimp, peeled and deveined
Sliced green onions, for garnish
Chopped parsley, for garnish
Cooked white rice

In a large skillet, melt butter over medium-low heat. Add flour, stirring continuously for 8-10 minutes to make a roux the color of peanut butter. Mix in onion and bell pepper; cook for 5 minutes. Add garlic and cook for 3 minutes more. Stir in stock, Mulate's Cajun Seasoning, salt, garlic powder, and bay leaf. Simmer for 20 minutes, stirring occasionally. Add shrimp and cook for 5-8 minutes, or until shrimp are pink. Remove bay leaf. Serve over cooked rice. Serves 6.

# Pesto Pasta with Sautéed Shrimp

*My dad taught me to make this delicious homemade pesto sauce, and it's a favorite of my two daughters. He always makes it for them! I like to add shrimp, but the sauce is so versatile, it goes with pretty much any protein.*

### PESTO PASTA WITH SAUTÉED SHRIMP

1 lb. 21/25 count shrimp, peeled and deveined
1 tbsp. Mulate's Cajun Seasoning
2 tbsp. extra virgin olive oil
1 lb. cooked pasta (I prefer linguini or spaghetti)
Parmesan cheese to top

Season shrimp with Mulate's Cajun Seasoning. In a skillet, heat the oil over medium heat. Sauté shrimp for 3 minutes on each side, or until pink and cooked through.

Toss cooked pasta with Pesto Sauce to coat. Transfer pasta to a plate and top with 6-8 shrimp. Garnish with freshly grated Parmesan cheese. Serves 6-8.

### PESTO SAUCE

½ cup pine nuts, lightly toasted
3 garlic cloves
½ tsp. kosher salt
⅔ cup extra virgin olive oil
3½ cups fresh basil leaves, tightly packed

Place pine nuts, garlic, and salt in a food processor and pulse until a paste forms. Be sure to scrape down the sides of the bowl. Add olive oil and pulse until combined. Add basil leaves and pulse to combine, scraping the sides of the bowl occasionally. Makes 1 cup. You will use approximately 1 cup of pesto to 1 lb. of pasta.

# New Orleans-Style Barbecued Shrimp

*Serve with warm French bread to sop up the buttery, delicious sauce!*

1 cup unsalted butter, melted
6 oz. Worcestershire sauce
4 lemons, juiced
3 tsp. Mulate's Cayenne Pepper Sauce
4 tsp. kosher salt
1 tbsp. fresh ground black pepper
1 tsp. rosemary
6 cloves garlic, roughly chopped
50 large headless shrimp, shells on
1 medium onion, sliced into rings
1 lemon, sliced into rounds
1 loaf fresh French bread

Preheat oven to 400 degrees. In a mixing bowl, mix to combine first 8 ingredients. Set aside.

Place shrimp in 11x13 baking dish. Top with onion and lemon slices. Pour butter mixture over shrimp. Bake 15 minutes. Remove dish from oven and stir. Return to oven and bake until shrimp are pink. Serves 6.

# Creamy Oyster Pasta

*Oysters are best when eaten from September through April. We still follow the rule—some consider it a myth—that oysters should not be eaten during months that do not contain an "r" (May through August).*

2 tbsp. unsalted butter
½ cup diced onion
¼ cup sliced green onion
3 cloves garlic, minced
1 cup white wine, like a Sauvignon Blanc
1 cup vegetable broth
3 cups heavy cream
1 bay leaf
1 tbsp. thyme
½ cup Parmesan cheese
4 dozen fresh oysters
1 tsp. kosher salt
½ tsp. white pepper
1 lb. cooked angel hair pasta

In a large skillet, melt butter over medium heat. Sauté onion and green onion for 3-5 minutes, or until soft. Add garlic and sauté for 1 minute more. Stir in white wine, and simmer for 2 minutes. Stir in broth, cream, bay leaf, and thyme. Stirring occasionally, simmer for 8 minutes to allow sauce to thicken. Add Parmesan and oysters and cook until oyster edges begin to curl. Remove and discard bay leaf. Season with salt and pepper. In a large bowl, gently toss cooked pasta and oyster sauce. Garnish with Parmesan. Serves 6.

Mulate's main dining room

# MEAT & POULTRY

# Roast

*This is my favorite roast to use for po' boys, but this crowd-pleaser can also be served over rice or with my Spicy New Potato Mash (see Index).*

4-5 lb. sirloin tip roast or eye of round roast
1 tbsp. Mulate's Cajun Seasoning
⅓ cup vegetable oil
3 cups diced onions
1 cup diced bell pepper
½ cup diced celery
2 cups beef broth
2 cups water
1 tsp. Mulate's Cajun Seasoning
Salt and pepper to taste

Season roast with Mulate's Cajun Seasoning. In a large pot, heat oil over medium heat. Brown the roast on all sides and remove from the pot. Add onions, bell pepper, and celery to the pot; sauté for 5 minutes. Add water and broth and season with Mulate's Cajun Seasoning and salt and pepper to taste. Simmer for 10 minutes, stirring occasionally. Return the roast to the pot. Cover and simmer over low heat for 90 minutes, stirring occasionally. Turn the roast and simmer for another 90 minutes, stirring occasionally. Slice or chop roast, then return to the pot to continue cooking for 30 minutes. When done, the roast will easily fall apart. Serves 10-12.

---

*Note:* When making po' boys, I prefer to use sirloin tip roast rather than eye of round roast.

# Roast Beef Debris Po' Boy

*A signature po' boy in New Orleans. The sloppier, the better!*

4 6-inch French bread pistolettes, halved lengthwise
Mayonnaise
1 lb. Roast, chopped
Gravy from roast
Shredded lettuce
Sliced tomatoes
Dill pickle rounds

In a skillet over medium heat, warm bread on both sides. Remove from heat and spread mayonnaise on both halves of bread. Layer chopped roast, gravy, lettuce, tomatoes, and pickles. Serves 4.

# Barbecued Beef Po' Boy

*When I was about 7 years old, my dad owned a sandwich shop in Bucktown, which is a little neighborhood just outside New Orleans. He served these delicious po' boys and when I take one bite today, it brings me back to my childhood.*

Monique and Maia enjoying Kerry's original recipe for Barbecued Beef Po' Boys.

1 lb. Roast, chopped (see Index)
2 cups Jack Miller's Barbecue Sauce
2 tbsp. Steen's Cane Syrup
4 6-inch French bread pistolettes, halved lengthwise
Mayonnaise
Shredded lettuce
Sliced tomatoes
Dill pickle rounds

Combine the chopped roast, barbecue sauce, and cane syrup in a saucepot over medium heat. Simmer for 5 minutes then remove from heat. In a skillet over medium heat, warm bread on both sides. Remove from heat and spread mayonnaise on both halves of bread. Layer barbecued beef, lettuce, tomatoes, and pickles. Serves 4.

# Pork Roast

*This is a good, easy recipe for pork roast. This roast can also be pulled and bathed in your favorite barbecue sauce to make pulled pork sandwiches. Be sure to use Mulate's Coleslaw (see Index) to top them!*

3 lb. Boston butt pork roast
1-2 tbsp. Mulate's Cajun Seasoning
1 tbsp. garlic powder
1 tsp. kosher salt
2 tbsp. vegetable oil
2 cups diced onions
1 cup diced bell pepper
3 cloves garlic, minced
2 cups water

Preheat oven to 325 degrees. Season the roast with Mulate's Cajun Seasoning, garlic powder, and salt. In a large oven-safe pot or Dutch oven, heat oil over medium heat. Brown the roast on both sides then remove from pot. Add onions and bell pepper; cook for 5 minutes, stirring frequently. Add garlic and cook for 3 minutes more. Add water and deglaze the pot by scraping all of the little browned bits to incorporate. Return roast to the pot. Cover and bake for 2½ hours.

Remove roast and discard any fat. Skim excess oil off gravy and bring to a simmer. In a small bowl, whisk 2 tbsp. cornstarch with 2 tbsp. cold water until incorporated. Stir cornstarch mixture into the pot. You will immediately see the gravy thicken. Return roast to the pot and simmer an additional 3-5 minutes. Serve over rice. Serves 8.

# Red Beans & Rice

*Originally made with pork bones left over from Sunday dinner, this traditional Creole dish is customarily made on Mondays. My husband's grandmother, Nana, always made it with pickled pork, and he grew up eating it regularly. This is one of my recipes inspired by Nana. She never used smoked sausage, but that is a staple in the Cajun kitchen. You can easily double this recipe. If you choose to double the recipe, use 3 cups of onions and 1½ cups of bell pepper.*

1 lb. pickled pork
2 cups diced onions
1 cup diced bell pepper
¼ cup diced celery
2 cloves garlic, minced
1½ tbsp. Mulate's Cajun Seasoning
2 tsp. salt
1 lb. red beans, rinsed and drained
6 cups water
4 cups reduced sodium chicken broth
1 lb. smoked sausage link, cut in half

In a medium pot, boil the pickled pork in water for 10 minutes. This will remove excess salt. Drain and set aside.

In a large pot over medium heat, cook onion, bell pepper, and celery for 15 minutes. Add garlic and cook for 3 minutes. Stir in Mulate's Cajun Seasoning and salt. Add pickled pork, beans, water, and broth. Cover and simmer over low heat for 2½-3 hours, stirring occasionally. Uncover and cook for 15 minutes.

Meanwhile, cut the smoked sausage links in half lengthwise. Brown the sausage in a skillet over medium-high heat. Drain excess grease on a paper towel. Serve sausage on top of the beans. Serve over cooked rice. Serves 8.

# Cajun Smothered Chicken

*This was a Sunday dinner staple in my grandmother Ida's kitchen. Tender and delicious, this is one of my personal favorites.*

3 chicken breasts, bone-in and skin-on
4 chicken thighs, bone-in and skin-on
1 tbsp. Mulate's Cajun Seasoning
3 tbsp. vegetable oil
2 cups diced onions
1 cup diced bell pepper
½ cup diced celery
4 cloves garlic, minced
1 tsp. kosher salt
3 cups reduced sodium chicken broth
1 cup water

Rinse, dry, and season chicken with Mulate's Cajun Seasoning. In a large pot, heat oil over medium heat. Working in batches, brown the chicken pieces on both sides, then remove them from the pan. Add onions, bell pepper, celery, garlic, and salt and cook for 5 minutes. Add ½ cup chicken broth and deglaze the pan by scraping all of the little browned bits to incorporate. Add the rest of the chicken broth and water and bring to a simmer. Add chicken pieces back to the pot, reduce heat to low, and cover. Cook for 2 hours, stirring occasionally. Skim excess oil. Serve over plain white rice or serve with gravy. Serves 8.

---

**To serve with gravy:** Remove the chicken pieces from the pan and pull the meat from the bones. Set meat aside and discard the bones. Whisk together 2 tbsp. cornstarch with 2 tbsp. cold water until smooth. Add the cornstarch mixture to the pot, stirring constantly over low heat until gravy thickens. Return chicken to the pot and bring to a simmer. Serve over rice.

# Panéed Chicken Breast

*These thin, lightly breaded chicken breasts pair well with buttered pasta and herbs. I also like them with my Arugula Salad (see Index).*

6 boneless, skinless chicken breasts
1 cup all-purpose flour
1 tsp. kosher salt
½ tsp. fresh cracked black pepper
2 large eggs
1¼ cups seasoned breadcrumbs
½ cup grated Parmesan cheese, plus extra for garnish
1 tbsp. unsalted butter
1 tbsp. extra virgin olive oil

Pound the chicken breasts until they are ¼-inch thick. In a shallow bowl or plate, combine the flour, salt, and pepper. In a separate bowl, whisk together the eggs. On a third plate, combine the breadcrumbs and the Parmesan cheese. Dredge each breast first in the flour mixture, then the eggs, and finally the breadcrumb mixture, coating both sides.

In a large skillet over medium heat, heat butter and olive oil. Sauté the chicken breasts for 3 minutes on each side, until cooked through and golden brown. Serves 6.

# Unstuffed Cabbage Rolls

*Quick, easy, and healthy—perfect for a weeknight dinner!*

1 lb. lean ground beef or turkey
1 cup diced onions
½ cup diced bell pepper
3 cloves garlic, minced
10 oz. can Ro-Tel diced tomatoes
8 oz. tomato sauce
1 tbsp. Mulate's Cajun Seasoning
2 tsp. garlic powder
1 tsp. salt or to taste
1 small head of cabbage, chopped

In a large skillet, brown ground meat over medium heat. Add onions and bell pepper and cook for 5 minutes. Add garlic, diced tomatoes, and tomato sauce; mix well. Stir in Mulate's Cajun Seasoning, garlic powder, and salt. Add chopped cabbage and cook for 20 minutes, or until cabbage has wilted and flavors have come together. Serves 6.

# Easy Lasagna

*This is a go-to recipe for me during the busy week. My daughters love it and will bring the leftovers to school for lunch the next day.*

2 tbsp. extra virgin olive oil
1 lb. lean ground turkey
½ cup diced shallots
3 cloves garlic, minced
½ tsp. red pepper flakes
10 oz. fresh spinach
1½ tsp. kosher salt
25 oz. jar of your favorite marinara sauce
8 oz. no-boil lasagna noodles
1½ cups grated Parmesan cheese
8 slices unsmoked provolone cheese
½ cup shredded mozzarella cheese

Preheat oven to 375 degrees. In a large oven-safe skillet, heat oil over medium heat. Brown the turkey. Mix in the shallots and garlic and cook for 3 minutes. Add red pepper flakes and spinach; cook for 3 minutes, or until spinach is wilted. Carefully transfer mixture to a large mixing bowl.

Spread ½ cup of marinara over the bottom of the skillet. Pour the remaining marinara into the mixing bowl and combine with the turkey mixture. Layer half the lasagna noodles on top of the marinara in the skillet. Layer half of the turkey mixture on top of the noodles. Add half the Parmesan cheese and 4 slices of provolone cheese. Repeat layers with the remaining noodles, turkey mixture, and cheeses. Top with shredded mozzarella.

Bake for 40 minutes. Cool for 5 minutes before serving. Serves 8.

# Frog Leg Sauce Piquante

*Fresh frog legs are hard to find these days, but if you can get them, you must make this dish!*

12 frog legs (approximately 1 lb.), rinsed
1 tsp. Mulate's Cajun Seasoning
2 tbsp. vegetable oil
1 cup diced onion
½ cup diced bell pepper
¼ cup diced celery
3 cloves garlic, minced
1 cup chicken broth
1 tbsp. tomato paste
10 oz. can Ro-Tel tomatoes
1 cup water

Season frog legs with Mulate's Cajun Seasoning. In a small Dutch oven, heat oil over medium heat. Brown the frog legs evenly on both sides and remove from the pot. Add onion, bell pepper, celery, and garlic and cook for 2-3 minutes. Stir in chicken broth; simmer for 5 minutes. Add tomato paste and tomatoes, continuing to cook for 5 minutes. Place frog legs back into the pot and add water. Cover and simmer over low heat for 30-40 minutes, stirring occasionally. Serve over rice. Serves 2-4.

Roasted Asparagus.

# VEGETABLES & SIDES

## Roasted Asparagus

*Asparagus is a favorite in our house. It is so easy to roast fresh asparagus and the dish comes out a beautiful bright green!*

1 bunch asparagus
Extra virgin olive oil
½ tsp. kosher salt
½ tsp. freshly cracked pepper
¼ cup freshly grated Parmesan cheese for garnish

Preheat oven to 400 degrees. Line a rimmed sheet pan with non-stick aluminum foil. Rinse asparagus and remove the tough lower part of the stems. Once asparagus spears have dried completely, spread evenly, in a single layer, on the prepared pan. Drizzle with olive oil and sprinkle with salt and pepper. Roast in oven for 10 minutes if your asparagus are pencil thin and 15 minutes if they are fatter. Garnish with cheese just before serving. Serves 4-6.

## Roasted Brussels Sprouts

*Even if you don't like Brussels sprouts, try this recipe. My daughters eat this like popcorn!*

3 cups fresh Brussels sprouts
2 tsp. extra virgin olive oil
½ tsp. kosher salt
½ tsp. freshly cracked pepper
Smoked paprika

Preheat oven to 400 degrees. Line a rimmed sheet pan with non-stick aluminum foil. Cut the Brussels sprouts in half and place in a mixing bowl. Add oil, salt, and pepper and toss to coat. Spread evenly on the prepared pan. Roast in the oven for 15 minutes. Shake and rotate the pan so that the Brussels sprouts brown evenly; cook for 5 minutes more. Remove from oven and sprinkle with smoked paprika. Serves 4-6.

Brussels Sprouts.

# Roasted Cauliflower & Broccoli with Pesto Sauce

*My Pesto Sauce is such a versatile sauce that it goes with everything—even vegetables!*

1 head broccoli, cut into florets
1 head cauliflower, cut into florets
3-4 tbsp. Pesto Sauce (see Index)
¼ cup shredded fresh Parmesan cheese

Preheat oven to 400 degrees. Line a rimmed sheet pan with non-stick aluminum foil. Spread the broccoli and cauliflower evenly on the prepared pan. Cook for 20 minutes. Remove from oven and transfer to a large bowl. Add Pesto Sauce and toss to coat. Garnish with grated Parmesan cheese. Serves 4-6.

## Herb-Roasted Broccoli

*I always like to have healthy options for side items. Playing around with seasonings is a great way to spice up your basic boiled or roasted broccoli.*

1 head of broccoli, cut into florets
1-2 tbsp. extra virgin olive oil
1 tsp. kosher salt
1 tsp. fresh ground black pepper
1 tsp. oregano
½ tsp. thyme leaves
½ tsp. rosemary

Preheat oven to 400 degrees. Line a rimmed sheet pan with non-stick aluminum foil. In a medium pot, bring water to a boil. Blanch broccoli florets for 3-5 minutes. Drain broccoli and transfer to a bowl. Add the remaining ingredients; stir well to combine. Spread broccoli evenly on the prepared pan. Bake for 10-15 minutes, until broccoli just starts to brown. Serves 4-6.

## Tarragon-Roasted Cauliflower

*I love the flavor of tarragon, and this is a great way to incorporate that flavor into a meal.*

1 head cauliflower, cut into florets
1 tbsp. unsalted butter
2 cloves garlic, minced
½ tsp. kosher salt
½ tsp. freshly cracked pepper
1 tbsp. tarragon
½ cup grated Parmesan cheese

Preheat oven to 400 degrees. Line a rimmed sheet pan with non-stick aluminum foil. In a large bowl, combine all ingredients except cheese. Spread seasoned cauliflower evenly on the prepared pan. Roast for 15 minutes. Garnish with Parmesan cheese. Serves 4.

## Stuffed Potatoes

*My daughter Maia's favorite side item! Omit the bacon for a meatless option*

2 large baking potatoes, rinsed
½ stick butter
1¼ cup shredded Cheddar cheese, divided
¼ cup chopped green onions
½ cup sour cream
4 strips cooked crispy bacon, crumbled
½ tsp. salt
¼ tsp. cayenne pepper

Preheat oven to 400 degrees. Wrap potatoes individually in aluminum foil. Bake for 75 minutes. Remove from oven, unwrap, and slice in half.

Reduce oven temperature to 350 degrees. Keeping the potato skin intact, scoop out potato flesh and transfer to a medium-sized bowl. Add butter and mix well. Add ¼ cup Cheddar cheese and remaining 5 ingredients; mix until well combined. Spoon potato mixture back into skins. Sprinkle remaining 1 cup Cheddar cheese over the potatoes. Bake for 15 minutes, or until cheese has melted. Serves 4.

## Spicy New Potato Mash

*You can also make this dish using your leftover crawfish boil potatoes.*

2 lb. red potatoes
1 pack crab boil
1 tsp. Mulate's Cajun Seasoning
½ cup heavy cream
Kosher salt to taste

In a large pot, boil potatoes in water seasoned with crab boil. Cook 20-30 minutes, or until tender. Drain and transfer potatoes to a large bowl. Using a potato masher, mash potatoes to your desired texture. Add Mulate's Cajun Seasoning and heavy cream; mix well. Add salt to taste. Serves 6-8.

## Sautéed Haricots Verts

*It is slightly more work to cook these fresh, but it's so worth it. If you're not a fan of thyme, simply leave it out!*

1 lb. fresh green beans, ends trimmed
1 tsp. unsalted butter
1 tsp. olive oil
½ cup diced shallots
2 cloves garlic, minced
½ tsp. dried thyme
Salt to taste
½ tsp. cayenne pepper

In a pot of boiling water, blanch green beans for 3 minutes. Drain and set aside. In a large skillet, heat butter and olive oil over medium heat. Add shallots and sauté for 3 minutes. Add garlic and sauté for 2 minutes. Stir in thyme, salt, and cayenne pepper. Add green beans and toss to coat. Serves 6.

## Baked Spirals & Cheese

*This creamy recipe is a little variation on your basic macaroni and cheese.*

1 lb. fusilli (spiral) pasta
2 tbsp. unsalted butter
⅔ cup Parmesan cheese
⅓ cup mozzarella cheese
⅓ cup Monterey Jack cheese
1 cup heavy cream
½ tsp. salt
¾ tsp. freshly cracked pepper

Preheat oven to 350 degrees. Boil the pasta in salted water until tender. Drain and transfer to a large bowl. Toss with butter and cheeses. Add cream, salt, and pepper; stir until well incorporated. Bake in a buttered 9x13 dish for 15-20 minutes, or until cheese is golden brown. Serves 6-8.

Blueberry Cobbler.

# SWEETS

## Blueberry Cobbler

*Blueberries are my favorite berry. I love making this cobbler in the spring and summer, at the peak of the season. Be sure to serve the cobbler warm with vanilla (or Creole cream cheese) ice cream on top!*

1¼ cups all-purpose flour
½ + ⅓ cup sugar, divided
¼ tsp. salt
1½ tsp. baking powder
¾ cup whole milk
⅓ cup butter, melted
2 cups fresh blueberries
1 tsp. vanilla extract

Preheat oven to 350 degrees. Butter an 8x8 baking dish. In a large mixing bowl, combine flour, ½ cup sugar, salt, and baking powder. Stir in milk and melted butter. Pour batter into prepared dish. In a separate bowl, mix together blueberries, ⅓ cup sugar, and vanilla extract. Spread blueberry mixture evenly over the top of the batter. Bake for 50 minutes or until a toothpick inserted in the middle comes out clean. Serves 6-8.

## Bananas Foster

*My dad's recipe for this famous New Orleans dessert!*

4 bananas
1½ sticks butter
¾ cup brown sugar
1 tsp. ground cinnamon
½ cup banana liqueur
½ cup rum
Vanilla ice cream

Cut the bananas in half, then cut them in half lengthwise. In a large saucepan, melt butter over medium heat. Add brown sugar and cinnamon, stirring constantly for 1 minute. Add bananas and banana liqueur, and cook bananas for 30 seconds on each side. The mixture should be simmering. Add rum then immediately remove from heat and light with a match. Carefully shake pan back and forth until flame goes out. Serve over ice cream. Serves 6-8.

# Lemon Icebox Pie

*This traditional southern dessert is best with freshly squeezed lemon juice. Since this is a variation of Key Lime Pie, you can easily substitute lime juice if you have fresh limes on hand.*

### VANILLA WAFER CRUST

½ cup unsalted butter, melted
2 cups finely crumbled vanilla wafers

Thoroughly mix melted butter into crumbled vanilla wafers. Press into a pie pan and chill for 30 minutes.

### FILLING

3 egg yolks
14 oz. condensed milk
½ cup freshly squeezed lemon juice
1 tsp. finely grated lemon zest
Whipped cream to top

Preheat oven to 300 degrees. Beat egg yolks with a hand mixer until light and fluffy. Stir in condensed milk. Slowly add lemon juice (the juice "cooks" the eggs and thickens the mixture). Stir in lemon zest. Pour into prepared Vanilla Wafer Crust. Bake for 30 minutes. Cool to room temperature then refrigerate for at least 4 hours before serving. Top with whipped cream. Serves 8.

# Pineapple-Coconut Bread Pudding

*I use my favorite flavors in this variation of Mulate's traditional bread pudding.*

6 eggs
6 oz. cream of coconut
2 cups half-and-half
1½ cups whole milk
½ cup sugar
8 oz. can crushed pineapple, drained (juice reserved for Tropical Rum Sauce)
6 hamburger buns
½ cup toasted coconut

Preheat oven to 350 degrees. Butter a 9x13 baking dish. In a large bowl, whisk eggs, cream of coconut, half-and-half, and milk. Add sugar and crushed pineapple; mix well. Break hamburger buns into pieces and spread in prepared pan. Sprinkle toasted coconut evenly throughout the bun pieces. Pour pineapple mixture over buns. Using your fingers, make sure that all bun pieces are soaked with the mixture. Bake for approximately 45 minutes. Top with Tropical Rum Sauce. Serves 8-10.

### TROPICAL RUM SAUCE

4 oz. cream of coconut
Reserved pineapple juice
½ cup half-and-half or heavy cream
½ cup coconut rum (or substitute plain rum)
2 tbsp. cornstarch mixed with 2 tbsp. cold water

In a small saucepan, simmer cream of coconut and pineapple juice over medium heat. Add half-and-half and rum and cook for 5 minutes. Stirring continuously, add cornstarch mixture to thicken the sauce. Serve over warm bread pudding.

## Pralines

*This recipe is inspired by my maternal grandmother, Leether, who taught me the "soft ball method." I don't use a candy thermometer, so I have to watch the candy closely as it cooks.*

- 2 cups white sugar
- 1 cup light brown sugar
- ¼ tsp. salt
- ½ cup condensed milk
- ¼ cup butter
- ½ cup whole milk
- 3 cups pecan halves

In a large saucepan, combine all ingredients except pecan halves. Slowly bring mixture to a boil over medium heat, stirring frequently. Boil until a small amount of the syrup forms a soft, pliable ball when dropped into water. This is the "soft ball method." Add pecan halves. Remove from heat and stir continuously for 3-5 minutes, or until creamy. Drop by spoonfuls onto wax paper. Let cool for 30 minutes. Makes 12 large pralines or 24 small pralines.

*Note:* Pralines are delicious by themselves, but you can also crumble pralines over vanilla ice cream for a wonderful dessert!

## Rich & Creamy Cheesecake

*The title of this recipe says it all.*

### CRUST
- ½ cup unsalted butter, melted
- 1 package vanilla wafers, crushed

Thoroughly mix melted butter into crushed vanilla wafers. Press into the bottom of 10-inch springform pan.

### FILLING
- 24 oz. cream cheese, softened
- ¾ cup sugar
- 2 tbsp. freshly squeezed lemon juice
- 3 large eggs, whisked

Preheat oven to 350 degrees. In a large mixing bowl, using a hand mixer, blend the cream cheese, sugar, and lemon juice. Add eggs and mix until well blended and smooth. Pour into crust and bake for 30 minutes. Remove from oven and let cool for 45 minutes.

### TOPPING
- 3 cups sour cream
- ¾ cup sugar
- 2 tsp. vanilla

Mix ingredients and pour over cooled cake. Return to 350-degree oven for 30 minutes. Remove from oven and cool to room temperature. Refrigerate 3 hours before serving. Serves 8.

Beautifully laid-out buffet in the Acadia Room at Mulate's.

# ENTERTAINING

This section of the book is dedicated to party planning and entertaining guests. I've included a party planning guide to use if you're throwing a party in your home. The two icons you see under each recipe title are for "Can Double" and for "Can Prepare in Advance." There is also a "Can Double" index at the back of the book for quick reference. The recipes at the front of the book are great substitutions if one of the menu items I've suggested doesn't work for your event. I'm hoping these ideas help you throw a fabulous party!

**Can Double**

**Can Prepare in Advance**

**One Month Before:**
— Set the date and time of the event.
— Create a guest list.
— Choose a theme, including décor, colors, and entertainment.

**Three Weeks Before:**
— Research food vendors and caterers. Did I mention that Mulate's caters?

**Two Weeks Before:**
— Send invitations.
— Create shopping lists for food and drinks.
— Place catering orders. My general rule of thumb for hors d'oeuvres is 3 bites per person.
— Enlist the help of family and friends.
— Order rental items.
— Shop for décor, tableware, and favors. If you're serving a gumbo or soup, remember to purchase bowls and spoons!

**One Week Before:**
— Shop for non-perishable groceries.
— Confirm with all helpers and vendors.

**Two Days Before:**
— Pick up rental items.
— Purchase all perishable items.
— Pick up fresh flowers . . . always a nice touch.

**One Day Before:**
— Prepare all food that can be made in advance.
— Begin decorating.
— Cut lemons and limes for your bar.
— Set up the bar and buffet areas, placing unopened bottles, empty ice buckets, platters, and bowls. Be sure you have space for everything.
— Set out cups, plates, napkins, and silverware.

**The Day of the Party:**
— Finish decorating.
— Complete food preparation.
— Pick up catering items.
— Turn on the music.
— Welcome guests and enjoy the party!

Set up your buffet so that guests start with the cold appetizers before progressing to hot appetizers then main items.

The Teche Room at Mulate's

## How to Stock a Bar

*When deciding how much alcohol to buy for a party, know your guests. What do they like? The type of alcohol you purchase is also determined by the type of party you're having. You wouldn't stock up on red wine for a brunch!*

**Wine and Champagne:**

- When buying bottles of wine and champagne, remember that each bottle holds 4-5 glasses. Purchase 1 bottle for every 2 guests who will be drinking wine.
- It's safe to say that you can get 6 glasses out of a bottle of champagne if you're mixing it with orange juice for mimosas.

**Beer:**

- When buying beer, assume 2-3 beers per each guest who will be drinking beer.

**Hard Liquor:**

- I'm of the opinion that you do not need a full bar at every home party; however, if you are planning on having a full bar, buy liter-size hard liquor for the best price.
- There are approximately 33 ounces in a liter. I always put a 1-ounce shot glass out on the bar to use for mixing cocktails. It's best if your guests don't just eyeball it! Accounting for those guests who like a stronger cocktail, you get about 25 drinks per liter of hard alcohol.
- Don't forget mixers if you're having a full bar. Items like club soda, cranberry juice, soft drinks, lemons, and limes are necessities.

If you're unsure of how much alcohol to purchase and what types to provide, and you would rather be safe than sorry, for every 10 guests you should purchase: 2 bottles of red wine and 2 bottles of white wine, a 12-pack of beer, 1 bottle of vodka, and 1 bottle of bourbon. Your guests will find something they like! And always keep a full pitcher of water, as well as water cups, on the bar for your guests.

Fun times in the Teche Room at Mulate's.

Learning to Cajun dance.

"In teaching the Cajun (Acadian) dance, we describe the music as one of the purest forms of 'root' music. We refer to the music as root music because the most important part of a living thing is its roots! Even our wonderful Cajun food is part of those roots and is mentioned in Cajun songs. Our history, our culture, our food are an integral part of Cajun music."—Paulette Barras, Mulate's Cajun Dance Instructor

"Thank you so much for everything! The total experience at Mulate's was excellent! I was totally impressed with you and your staff. The food and service were very good! We will strongly recommend Mulate's to our friends and family for future endeavors in NOLA."
—Sharon & Steve, Memphis, Tennessee

"It was such a pleasure having our rehearsal dinner there! You wouldn't believe the compliments we've gotten . . . and, oh, the food!! Wow! It was delicious! It was a pleasure meeting you. You are so sweet and helped us out so much along the way. We are truly thankful for your hard work and kindness!"
—Emily, Scott, Louisiana

"The food was excellent and the space was catered to our exact needs! But what I really cannot say enough wonderful things about is the service! Every one of your staff members was so polite and helpful. Anything we needed was provided right away, sometimes with the staff anticipating our needs before we even had to say anything! It was truly exceptional. Due to the success of the evening, we plan to make this a yearly event. I hope to be working with you again next year! Thanks again for a great experience!"—Michelle, LaPlace, Louisiana

Brunch at home.

# BRUNCH

Sunday (and sometimes Saturday) late mornings are for brunch. As a child growing up in the '80s in south Louisiana, I had never heard of brunch. Today, it's one of my favorite meals in New Orleans or wherever our travels take us. It's also my favorite party to throw. Although I prepare most of the items on the menu in my kitchen, I always like to pick up fresh French pastries from my local bakery. My suggested menu is easy for an at-home party, and Shrimp & Grits is a favorite of clients requesting a fabulous brunch in one of our private rooms at Mulate's. A brunch is always a fantastic idea for a bridal shower, a post-wedding gathering, or a baby shower.

### ~Menu~
Champagne Punch
Deviled Eggs
Spicy Smoked Tuna Dip
Pecan Mini Muffins
Shrimp & Grits
Yogurt Parfait

# Champagne Punch

*This is my absolute favorite drink to serve at brunch. Everyone is always nicely surprised when they taste that hint of pineapple juice!*

1 cup sliced strawberries
1 cup blueberries
⅓ cup Grand Marnier
2 cups orange juice
1 cup pineapple juice
1 liter ginger ale
2 bottles of dry champagne (750 mL each), chilled

Place strawberries and blueberries in a large pitcher. Pour Grand Marnier over the fruit. Refrigerate for at least 4 hours. Stir in the orange juice and pineapple juice. When ready to serve, gently stir in ginger ale and champagne. Serves 12-15.

# Deviled Eggs

*This is a great basic recipe. Feel free to add a little sweet relish, dill relish, sriracha sauce, bacon bits, or anything else you like.*

1 dozen large eggs, boiled and peeled
¼ cup mayonnaise
1 tbsp. Dijon mustard
2 tsp. white vinegar
1 tsp. Mulate's Cayenne Pepper Sauce
¼ tsp. cayenne pepper
Thinly sliced chives, for garnish

Cut boiled eggs in half lengthwise. Scoop out yolks and transfer to a bowl; set aside egg whites on a plate. Mash the yolks with the back of a fork. In a separate mixing bowl, combine the mayonnaise, mustard, vinegar, pepper sauce, and cayenne pepper. Add the mashed yolks to the mixture and stir until smooth and creamy. Transfer yolk mixture to a quart-sized plastic bag. Cut the bottom corner to create a hole and pipe the mixture into the egg whites. Top each with chives. Makes 24.

## Spicy Smoked Tuna Dip

*No meat smoker needed for this recipe!*

13 oz. vacuum-sealed albacore tuna
8 oz. cream cheese, softened
2 tbsp. liquid smoke
1 tbsp. Worcestershire sauce
1 tsp. garlic powder
½ tsp. cayenne pepper

Using a hand mixer on medium speed, combine all ingredients. Serve with crackers, pita chips, or vegetables. Serves 10.

## Pecan Mini Muffins

*These little bites are always a crowd-pleaser and are so easy to make!*

1 cup light brown sugar
1 cup chopped pecans
½ cup flour
2 eggs, whisked
1 stick unsalted butter, melted

Preheat oven to 350 degrees. In a medium bowl, mix together brown sugar, chopped pecans, and flour. Add eggs and butter and mix well. Spoon by teaspoons into mini muffin tins lined with mini muffin papers. Bake for 15-18 minutes. Makes 24 mini muffins.

# Shrimp & Grits

*My favorite menu item for brunch! This recipe is so quick and easy that your friends will think you spent hours in the kitchen. I like using the smaller shrimp because they are tasty and bite-sized; no knives needed.*

4 tbsp. unsalted butter
¼ cup flour
1 cup diced onions
½ cup diced bell pepper
¼ cup diced celery
2 cloves garlic, minced
1½ lb. 40/50 peeled and deveined shrimp
1 tbsp. Mulate's Cajun Seasoning
1 tsp. kosher salt
2¾ cups vegetable stock
¼ cup heavy cream
¼ cup sliced green onions
1 tbsp. chopped fresh parsley

In a large skillet, melt butter over medium-low heat. Add flour and cook, stirring constantly for 8-10 minutes to make a roux the color of peanut butter. Add onion, bell pepper, and celery and cook until soft, about 8 minutes. Add garlic and cook for 2 minutes. Fold in shrimp, Mulate's Cajun Seasoning, and salt. Stir in stock and cream. Simmer for 10 minutes, or until sauce thickens. Sauce should coat the back of a spoon. Remove from heat and toss in green onions and parsley. Serve over Quick Cheese Grits. Serves 8.

**QUICK CHEESE GRITS**
2 cups water
2 cups whole milk
1 cup quick cooking grits
2 cups shredded Monterey Jack cheese
1 tsp. garlic powder
½ tsp. cayenne pepper
2 tbsp. unsalted butter

In a large saucepan, bring water and milk to a gentle boil over medium heat. Stir in the grits. Return to a boil and cook for 4-5 minutes. Reduce heat to low and add cheese, stirring constantly until cheese is melted. Add garlic powder, cayenne pepper, and butter; stir to combine. Keep warm until ready to serve. Serves 8.

# Yogurt Parfait

*A simple and beautiful addition to your brunch spread. Serve them in small, pretty glasses.*

4 cups plain Greek yogurt
⅓ cup honey
2 tsp. vanilla extract
¼ cup freshly squeezed orange juice
1 tbsp. chopped mint leaves
2 cups fresh blueberries
1 cup sliced fresh strawberries

In a mixing bowl, combine yogurt, honey, and vanilla extract. In a separate mixing bowl, combine orange juice and mint leaves. Add berries and toss. Spoon the yogurt into small glasses, then add a layer of the berry mixture. Repeat yogurt layer and top with berry mixture. Serves 8.

# CRAWFISH BOIL

Are crawfish running yet? That's the question south Louisiana residents start asking after Thanksgiving. Is it going to be a long or short season? Did we get the right amount of rain to have a good season? If we are lucky, live crawfish will be in season through mid-May, so we can have that last boil on Mother's Day before the shells get too hard.

Although the main event at any crawfish boil is the crawfish, it's nice to have other items to nibble on while you're waiting for the crawfish to hit the table. It's also a great time to try out local craft beers because boiled crawfish go best with an ice-cold beer. This menu is what we offer in our private rooms when we have a client requesting a crawfish boil.

### ~Menu~

White Sangria
Boiled Crawfish
Mini Po' Boys
Spinach & Artichoke Dip
Mulate's Chicken & Sausage Jambalaya
Mulate's Homemade Bread Pudding

# White Sangria

*The sweetness of this sangria pairs well with spicy foods, but watch out . . . This one has a kick!*

2 cups St-Germain elderflower liqueur
½ cup Grand Marnier
1 cup sliced strawberries
1 cup raspberries
1 orange, halved and sliced
2 peaches, halved and sliced
2 bottles Pinot Grigio (750 mL), chilled

In a large pitcher, combine St-Germain, Grand Marnier, and fruit. Refrigerate for 4 hours. Stir in chilled wine and serve over ice. Makes 12 cups.

Crawfish soaking in the seasoned water.

# Boiled Crawfish

*This is my husband Murphy's recipe. It's a combination of the New Orleans-style method, with dry seasonings in the boil water, and Cajun-style preparation, with dry seasonings sprinkled on the crawfish once they're cooked.*

1 sack crawfish (35 lb.)
10 lemons, quartered
3 onions, quartered
3 heads garlic
8 cups Cajun Land Complete Boil
3 oranges, quartered
3 lb. small red potatoes
8 ears of corn, cut in half
1 pt. white mushrooms
2 cups Myran's Cajun Seafood Boil

Rinse the crawfish prior to boiling them. Pick out any grass, bait, or dead crawfish when you rinse them. It may take a few rinses to be sure they are clean, but it's a step not to be skipped!

In an extra-large pot filled with 9 gallons of water, add lemons, onions, garlic, Cajun Land seasoning, oranges, and potatoes. Bring to a rolling boil. Add crawfish and return to a boil. Once water begins to boil, turn off heat and add corn and mushrooms. The crawfish will rise to the top of the pot. Hose the outside of the pot with cool water for 5 minutes in order to cool the pot and stop the crawfish from continuing to cook. Let crawfish and seasonings soak for 30 minutes. The crawfish will fill with the seasoned water and sink. Drain the crawfish and seasonings. Transfer the crawfish to an empty ice chest. Separate the vegetables and set aside to serve. Sprinkle the Myran's seasoning over the crawfish and mix until seasoning is spread evenly throughout. Serves 6-8.

---

*To serve:* Cover a long table with one layer of garbage bags and a few layers of newspaper. Pour crawfish over the center of the table and dig in!

*Note:* If you are boiling multiple sacks, you can use the same seasoned water for up to 3 sacks of crawfish. Remember to rinse each sack before boiling.

Always have side items available at your boil.

## Mini Po' Boys

*These little sandwiches are an easy crowd-pleaser. Get fresh French bread the morning of your party. The fresh bread makes all the difference!*

3 loaves (10-12 inches each) French bread
Mayonnaise
1 lb. deli sliced smoked turkey
1 lb. deli sliced ham
1 lb. deli sliced roast beef
1 head iceberg lettuce, shredded
3 tomatoes, sliced
Pickle rounds

Cut loaves of French bread lengthwise. Coat one side of each loaf lightly with mayonnaise. On the first loaf, layer smoked turkey, lettuce, tomato slices, and pickles. Close the po' boy and cut into 10 individual pieces. Repeat this process with the ham and the roast beef. Makes about 10 mini po' boys per loaf or 30 mini po' boys overall.

## Spinach & Artichoke Dip

*Arguably one of the best hot dips there is. Ours has plenty of spinach, just the way I like it!*

1 stick unsalted butter
½ cup flour
1 cup diced onions
2 cloves garlic, minced
4 cups whole milk
1 cup grated Parmesan cheese
1 cup shredded Monterey Jack cheese
⅓ cup sour cream
1 tbsp. freshly squeezed lemon juice
2 tsp. Mulate's Cayenne Pepper Sauce
14 oz. can artichoke hearts, drained
40 oz. frozen chopped spinach, thawed
1 tbsp. Mulate's Cajun Seasoning
¼ tsp. cayenne pepper
½ tsp. salt, or to taste
1 cup shredded Monterey Jack cheese, for topping

Preheat oven to 350 degrees. Butter a 9x13 baking dish. Melt butter in a large Dutch oven over medium heat. Add flour and stir to combine. Cook for 3-5 minutes to make a blonde roux. Add onion and cook for 3 minutes. Add garlic and cook for 2 minutes. Add milk slowly, in a steady stream, stirring constantly to combine. While continuing to stir, bring mixture to a simmer. Add cheeses and stir to melt. Add sour cream, lemon juice, and Mulate's Cajun Pepper Sauce; stir to combine. Add artichoke hearts, spinach, Mulate's Cajun Seasoning, and cayenne pepper and mix well until completely combined. Pour into prepared baking dish and top with cheese. Bake for 35-40 minutes, or until bubbly. Let dip sit for 5 minutes before serving. Serves 15.

# Mulate's Chicken & Sausage Jambalaya

*Jambalaya is a perfect crowd-pleasing party food, and this recipe is easy to upsize for a crowd! You can double everything in the recipe, except the onions and bell pepper. When doubling, use 6 cups of diced onions and 2 cups of diced bell pepper.*

1 lb. boneless, skinless chicken thighs
1 lb. boneless, skinless chicken breasts
2 tbsp. Mulate's Cajun Seasoning
1 tbsp. vegetable oil
2 sticks unsalted butter
2 cups water
5 cups diced onions
1 cup diced bell pepper
3 cloves garlic, diced
1 lb. smoked sausage, sliced in ½-inch rounds
1 pt. fresh mushrooms, sliced
10 oz. can Ro-Tel diced tomatoes
4 cups cooked rice
¼ cup chopped green onions

Season all chicken pieces with Mulate's Cajun Seasoning. In a large Dutch oven, heat vegetable oil over medium-high heat. Working in batches so as not to overcrowd the pot, brown chicken on both sides. Remove chicken from pot and cut into bite-sized pieces. Set aside. Add butter, ½ cup water, and diced onions to pot. Be sure to scrape all the browned bits from the bottom and sides of the pot. Cook onions over medium heat for 30-40 minutes, until dark golden brown. Add water as needed to prevent sticking. Add bell pepper and garlic. Cook for 15 minutes, stirring frequently. Add chicken, sausage, mushrooms, Ro-Tel tomatoes, and any remaining water to pot. Reduce heat to medium-low and continue cooking for 45 minutes, stirring occasionally. Fold in cooked rice. Toss in green onions and mix well. Serves 8-10.

# Mulate's Homemade Bread Pudding

*A customer favorite! Bread pudding is our all-time best-selling dessert. This ultimate comfort food has been around for centuries. According to food historians, this "poor man's pudding" was originally created so as not to waste stale bread. This is our founder Kerry Boutté's recipe as he made it when he opened Mulate's in Breaux Bridge in 1980. The secret ingredient is hamburger buns . . . and they don't have to be stale. You can also be creative and substitute whatever you like for the raisins. One of my friends uses this recipe to make bread pudding around the holidays. She omits the raisins and adds Nutella. Yummm!*

6 eggs
1 tsp. vanilla extract
2 cups whole milk
2 cups half-and-half
1 cup sugar
6 hamburger buns
½ cup raisins

Preheat oven to 350 degrees. Butter a 9x13 baking dish. In a large bowl, whisk eggs, then add vanilla, milk, and half-and-half. Add sugar and mix well. Break hamburger buns into chunks and place in greased pan. Sprinkle raisins evenly throughout the bun pieces. Pour egg mixture over buns. Using your fingers, make sure that all bun pieces are soaked with the mixture. Bake for approximately 45 minutes. If you prefer a firmer texture, chill for about 2 hours, then reheat for serving. Top with Butter Rum Sauce. Serves 10.

### BUTTER RUM SAUCE

½ stick unsalted butter
¼ cup sugar
½ cup half-and-half or heavy cream
½ cup rum

In a small skillet, melt butter over medium heat. Add sugar and cook for 3 minutes. Add half-and-half (or cream) and rum. Cook for 5 minutes or until slightly thickened. Serve warm over Mulate's Homemade Bread Pudding.

Sunday lunch just like Ida's.

# SUNDAY LUNCH

As a child, we would go to my grandmother Ida's for Sunday lunch. She ate early, at 11 A.M. sharp. Sunday lunch is one of my fondest memories of my grandmother as she would always have lots of stories to tell. She and my dad would switch back and forth between English and French, depending on whether or not they wanted me to know what they were saying. My grandfather, Ram, was pretty quiet and spoke French most of the time. The entire tip of his pinkie finger had been cut off in an accident, and he would tease me by acting like he was going to tickle me under my chin with his little pinkie. The thought makes me giggle even today.

### *~Menu~*

Mint Iced Sweet Tea
Sliced Tomatoes & Mayonnaise
Smothered Seven Steaks
Corn Macque Choux
Sock It to Me Cake

## Mint Iced Sweet Tea

*This is my addition to Ida's Sunday lunch menu.*

8 cups filtered water
12 tea bags
10 mint leaves
1 cup sugar

In a medium pot, bring water to a rolling boil over high heat. Remove from heat and add tea bags and mint leaves. Steep for 15 minutes. Carefully remove tea bags and mint leaves. Add sugar and stir until completely dissolved. Once tea has cooled, pour into a pitcher and refrigerate for at least 3 hours. Serve over ice. Makes 8 cups.

## Sliced Tomatoes & Mayonnaise

*My grandfather had a vegetable garden in his backyard. When the tomatoes were plentiful, we would have simple sliced tomatoes with a little dollop of mayonnaise on the side with our Sunday lunch.*

2-3 tomatoes, sliced
Salt and pepper to taste
Mayonnaise

Place 3-4 tomato slices on each plate. Sprinkle with salt and pepper. Top with a spoonful of mayonnaise. Serves 6.

Three generations.

Kerry and his granddaughters, Maia and Renée.

# Smothered Seven Steaks "Rice 'n Gravy"

*This is a traditional Cajun Sunday dinner. I've enjoyed "rice 'n gravy" for as long as I can remember, but this dish is neither low in fat nor "heart healthy" so I had stopped cooking it for my family. Last year, I was having a discussion with friends about heritage and family recipes, and I realized that my daughters did not know what "rice 'n gravy" is because I hadn't cooked it in so long! I actually needed a little help to remember how to make it. Well, once my family tasted this deliciousness, they requested that it be placed on the dinner rotation. I acquiesced, but I only serve it once a month instead of once a week. I told my daughters that this is one they have to learn to cook so the recipe will live on. In a time when we are always in a rush to make dinner, take your time with this one. It's worth it!*

2-2½ lb. seven steaks, bone-in if possible
1 tbsp.+2 tsp. Mulate's Cajun Seasoning, divided
¼ cup vegetable oil
1 tsp. kosher salt
2 cups diced onions
1 cup diced bell pepper
2 cloves garlic, minced

Season seven steaks with 1 tbsp. Mulate's Cajun Seasoning. In a large pot, heat oil over medium-high heat. Working in batches so as not to crowd the pot, brown the meat for 5 minutes on each side. You want to brown the meat well because this is the base for your gravy. This process will take 20-25 minutes. Once all the meat is browned and the last batch is removed from the pot, add onions and bell pepper. Sauté for 5 minutes then add ½ cup water to deglaze the pot. Be sure to scrape all the brown tidbits that were left behind from browning the meat. Reduce heat to medium and simmer for 5 minutes. Stir in garlic, 2 tsp. Mulate's Cajun Seasoning, and kosher salt. Stir in ½ cup water and cook for 5 minutes. Repeat this process twice more: add ½ cup water and let the vegetables cook down for 5 minutes. This process is a bit tedious, but you are working on a delicious gravy! Add meat back into pot and add enough water to cover. Reduce heat to low, cover, and simmer for 2 hours, stirring occasionally. Skim any excess oil. Season to taste. Serves 6.

---

*To serve:* Rice 'n gravy pairs perfectly with corn macque choux; I like to mix the corn in with the rice once it's served on the plate.

*Note:* If you would like to double this recipe, use 3 cups of diced onions and 1½ cups diced bell peppers.

# Corn Macque Choux

*My grandmother made this every Sunday for lunch. It's a traditional Cajun side dish that goes well with Rice 'n Gravy.*

9 ears fresh corn
1 cup diced onions
½ cup diced bell pepper (red or green or a little bit of both!)
½ small tomato, peeled and diced
1 tsp. Mulate's Cajun Seasoning
¼ cup vegetable oil

With a sharp knife, cut the corn off the cob. Using the blunt edge of the knife, scrape the cob over a mixing bowl to collect all of the juices, then combine corn, bell pepper, tomato, and Mulate's Cajun Seasoning with the juice. Heat oil in a large pot over medium-high heat. Add corn mixture, reduce heat to medium, and cook for 10 minutes, stirring frequently. Cover and simmer over low heat for 2 hours. Stir every 15 minutes. When the corn begins to stick to the bottom of the pot, add ¼ cup water and scrape to deglaze. Serves 6-8.

---

*Note:* If fresh corn isn't in season, you can substitute 4 cans of whole kernel corn.

# Sock It to Me Cake

*This is my variation of my grandmother Ida's recipe.*

½ cup+1 tbsp. sugar
½ cup unsalted butter
4 eggs
½ pt. sour cream
1 box yellow butter cake mix, sifted
5 tbsp. chopped pecans
4 tbsp. light brown sugar
1 tbsp. cocoa powder

**ICING**
1 cup confectioner's sugar, sifted
2 tbsp. unsalted butter, melted
2 tbsp. warm milk
1 tsp. vanilla extract

Combine all ingredients; mix well.

Preheat oven to 350 degrees. Prepare baking pan or Bundt pan with non-stick spray or butter and flour. Using a hand mixer, cream together ½ cup sugar and butter. Add eggs one at a time, mixing well. Add sour cream and mix until well incorporated. Add cake mix. Beat batter for 4 minutes. In a separate bowl, combine pecans, brown sugar, cocoa powder, and 1 tbsp. sugar to make a filling. Pour half of cake batter into prepared pan. Sprinkle the filling over the batter as the next layer. Top with remaining batter. Bake for 40-45 minutes. Drizzle with icing while still warm. Serves 12-15.

Putting together the perfect Game Day menu.

# GAME DAY PARTY

In my house "Game Day" always refers to friends, drinks, and SEC football. Both my husband and I attended LSU, and football games were a big part of our college lives. Game Day is different for everyone, depending on which part of the country you're from. This menu works well wherever your Game Day may be.

*~Menu~*

Painkiller
Cajun-Style Party Mix
French Muffaletta
Hot Buffalo Chicken Dip
Chili
Chocolate Sheet Cake

## Painkiller

*We discovered this drink while on vacation in the British Virgin Islands. Pusser's Rum is the secret ingredient. One sip and you're on the beach in White Bay!*

2 cups Pusser's Rum
4 oz. cream of coconut
2 cups pineapple juice
1 cup orange juice
Grated fresh nutmeg, essential garnish
Orange slices for garnish
Maraschino cherries for garnish

In a large pitcher, mix rum, cream of coconut, and juices. Refrigerate for 1 hour. Stir well. Pour into cocktail glasses over ice and top with fresh grated nutmeg, orange slices, and cherries. Serves 6.

## Cajun-Style Party Mix

*Of course you can buy party mix at the store, but the homemade version is so much better! This mix also makes great teacher or holiday gifts. I like savory, spicy flavors, but if you prefer a sweet and spicy mix, use 1 cup of honey-roasted peanuts in place of 1 cup of mixed nuts.*

1½ sticks unsalted butter
3½ tbsp. Worcestershire sauce
2 tsp. Mulate's Cayenne Pepper Sauce
3 tsp. Mulate's Cajun Seasoning
½ tsp. garlic powder
½ tsp. onion powder
3 cups Corn Chex
3 cups Rice Chex
3 cups Wheat Chex
2 cups mixed nuts
2 cups bite-sized cheese crackers
1 cup bite-sized pretzels

Preheat oven to 250 degrees. Melt butter in a large roasting pan placed in the oven. When butter has melted, remove pan and stir in sauces and seasonings. Fold in remainder of ingredients and toss to coat. Roast for 1 hour, stirring every 15 minutes. Spread on paper towels to dry completely. Makes 14 cups.

# French Muffaletta

*We had so many customers come into the restaurant and request a muffaletta that we decided to make our own and put a French spin on the New Orleans Italian favorite! This recipe is for a whole sandwich, but simply cut it into smaller pieces to serve at a party.*

1 loaf French bread, sliced lengthwise
Olive salad mix
½ lb. sliced ham
½ lb. sliced provolone cheese
½ lb. sliced Genoa salami

On one side of the sliced French bread, spread olive salad mix. Layer ham, provolone, and salami. On the other side of the loaf, spread a little bit of olive oil from the olive salad mix. Press sandwich together and slice as you like. We use a panini press to heat ours before serving. Serves 2 as a meal or 12 as an appetizer.

# Hot Buffalo Chicken Dip

*Creamy and spicy—a perfect, easy substitute for buffalo wings!*

8 oz. cream cheese, softened
1 oz. packet ranch dressing seasoning mix
16 oz. sour cream
2 cups shredded Cheddar cheese, plus more for topping
2 cups shredded rotisserie chicken
¼ cup buffalo sauce
2 tsp. Mulate's Cayenne Pepper Sauce
Sliced chives for garnish

Preheat oven to 375 degrees. In a large mixing bowl, combine all ingredients except chives. Mix well. Pour into a buttered pie plate and cover with foil. (If you are preparing this dip in advance, place the dish in the refrigerator at this point.) Bake for 20 minutes. Remove from oven and sprinkle cheese on top. Return to oven and bake for 10 minutes. Garnish with chives. Serve immediately with corn chips, carrot rounds, and celery sticks. Serves 10.

# Chili

*The cinnamon adds an additional layer of flavor in this meaty chili. In our house, chili is always served with your choice of corn chips, shredded Cheddar cheese, sour cream, and green onions!*

1 tbsp. extra virgin olive oil
1 lb. ground meat of your choice
2 cups diced onions
½ jalapeno, minced
8 cloves garlic, minced
10 oz. can Ro-Tel diced tomatoes
2 tbsp. cumin
2 tbsp. chili powder
2 tsp. kosher salt
½ tsp. smoked paprika
¼ tsp. cinnamon
15 oz. tomato sauce
1½ cups chicken, beef, or vegetable broth
14 oz. can great northern beans
14 oz. can black beans

In a soup pot, heat the oil and brown the ground meat over medium heat. Drain fat, if necessary. Add onions and sauté for 5 minutes. Mix in jalapeno, garlic, diced tomatoes, and dry seasonings; cook for 5 minutes. Stir in tomato sauce and broth. Cook for 20 minutes. Add beans and cook for 20 minutes more. Serves 8.

# Chocolate Sheet Cake

*Who doesn't love a good chocolate sheet cake? This cake isn't too sweet by itself, so the fudge icing is a great complement. You can omit the pecans for a nut-free icing.*

2 cups flour
2 cups sugar
2 sticks unsalted butter
1 cup water
4 tbsp. cocoa powder
1 tsp. vanilla extract
1 tsp. baking soda
½ cup half-and-half
2 eggs, whisked

Preheat oven to 350 degrees. Prepare a 9x13 baking pan with non-stick spray or butter and flour. In a mixing bowl, sift together flour and sugar. In a small saucepot, bring butter, water, and cocoa powder to a boil. Pour butter mixture into flour mixture, and stir to combine. Add vanilla, baking soda, and half-and-half; mix well. Add eggs and stir until thoroughly combined. Pour into prepared baking pan. Bake for 45 minutes. Top with Chocolate Pecan Fudge Icing.

### CHOCOLATE PECAN FUDGE ICING

1 stick unsalted butter
4 tbsp. cocoa powder
⅓ cup half-and-half

1 box confectioner's sugar
1 tsp. vanilla extract
1 cup pecans

In a medium saucepot, melt butter over medium-high heat. Stir in cocoa and half-and-half. Cook for 5 minutes. Remove from heat, then add confectioner's sugar and pecans. Mix well. Spread over cake while both icing and cake are hot.

Celebrating Claudette's 70th birthday in the Teche Room at Mulate's.

# DINNER PARTY

This menu works well when you want to celebrate. Even when you've had a long week and just don't feel like going out to dinner, this is the perfect menu for having some friends over.

### ~Menu~

Red Sangria
Arugula Salad
Braised Short Ribs
Creamed Spinach
Garlic Bread
Fluffy Cheesecake with Blueberry Sauce

Red Sangria.

## Red Sangria

*If you don't have any brandy, add another cup of apple juice. You and your guests will still enjoy every sip of this classic sangria.*

1 cup brandy
1 orange, halved and sliced
1 green apple, halved and sliced
2 cups orange juice
1 cup apple juice
2 bottles dry red wine

In a large pitcher, stir together brandy, orange slices, and apple slices. Refrigerate for 4 hours. Stir in orange juice, apple juice, and wine. Serve over ice. Makes 12 cups.

## Arugula Salad

*I love the peppery flavor of arugula, and this simple salad is always a hit!*

½ cup freshly squeezed lemon juice
1 cup extra virgin olive oil
1 tsp. kosher salt
½ tsp. freshly cracked black pepper
1 lb. fresh arugula, rinsed and dried
½ lb. Parmesan cheese

In a small mixing bowl, whisk together lemon juice, olive oil, salt, and pepper to make a dressing. Pour dressing over the arugula and toss. Transfer to serving plates and shave pieces of Parmesan over the top. Serves 8-10.

Braised Short Ribs.

# Braised Short Ribs

*I don't eat beef often, but my favorite beef dish is this recipe for short ribs. You can prepare this dish a day in advance. The flavors really come together after sitting in the refrigerator overnight.*

5 lb. boneless beef short ribs
2-3 tbsp. Mulate's Cajun Seasoning
¼ cup vegetable oil
3 cups diced onions
½ cup diced carrots
¼ cup diced celery
4 cups low sodium beef broth, divided
4 cloves garlic, minced
1 cup Cabernet Sauvignon
2 tbsp. Worcestershire sauce
2 tsp. thyme
2 tbsp. cornstarch
2 tbsp. cold water
Salt and pepper to taste

Preheat oven to 350 degrees. Season short ribs with Mulate's Cajun Seasoning. Heat oil over medium heat in a large oven-safe pot. Working in batches, brown the short ribs on both sides. Remove browned short ribs from pot and set aside. Add onions, carrots, celery, and ½ cup beef broth. Cook for 3 minutes. Mix in garlic and cook for 2 more minutes. Add the remaining beef broth, Cabernet Sauvignon, Worcestershire sauce, and thyme; bring to a simmer. Return the short ribs to the pot. Cover and bake for 2½ hours.

Remove the short ribs from the pot. Skim excess oil and bring gravy to a simmer over medium heat. Whisk together 2 tbsp. cornstarch and 2 tbsp. cold water. Add cornstarch mixture to gravy, stirring constantly until incorporated. You will immediately see the gravy thicken. Add the short ribs back into pot and simmer for 3-5 minutes. Add salt and pepper to taste. Serves 8-10.

---

*To serve:* You can serve your short ribs with mashed potatoes, rice, or my personal favorite, Quick Cheese Grits (see Index).

*Note:* If you prefer not to use wine, you can substitute 1 cup of water in its place.

## Creamed Spinach

*You can use frozen spinach to save time, but if you're looking to impress your guests, fresh spinach really makes this side outstanding.*

2 lb. baby spinach
4 tbsp. unsalted butter
¼ cup diced shallots
1 clove garlic, minced
1 tsp. kosher salt
¼ cup flour
1⅓ cups whole milk
¼ cup shredded Monterey Jack cheese
¼ cup grated Parmesan cheese

In a large pot of boiling water, blanch spinach for 3 minutes. Strain through a fine mesh strainer to remove water. Set aside.

In a sauce pot, melt butter over medium heat. Add shallots and sauté for 3 minutes, just until softened. Add garlic and sauté for 2 minutes. Add salt and flour, stirring constantly to form a blonde (light) roux. Add milk in a slow, steady stream, stirring to incorporate. Bring to a simmer then add both cheeses. Stir well to incorporate. Fold spinach into melted cheese mixture. Serves 8.

## Garlic Bread

*If you want each piece of bread to be very crunchy, similar to a crouton, cut the pieces before you bake them.*

1 loaf (10-12 inches) French bread
6 tbsp. unsalted butter
1 head garlic, peeled and minced
½ cup fresh chopped parsley
½ cup grated Parmesan cheese, optional

Preheat oven to 350 degrees. Slice the loaf in half lengthwise. In a small pot, melt butter over medium heat. Sauté minced garlic. Turn off heat and let sit for 30 minutes to cool. Spread the garlic butter on the French bread. Top with parsley and Parmesan cheese. Place on baking sheet and bake for 15 minutes. Serves 12-15.

# Fluffy Cheesecake with Blueberry Sauce

*Although everyone in my house loves this cheesecake, I perfected this recipe for EB, so he gets a piece every time I make it.*

### CRUST
4 tbsp. unsalted butter, melted
2 cups graham cracker crumbs

Thoroughly mix melted butter into graham cracker crumbs. Press into a 10-inch springform pan. Set aside.

### CHEESECAKE
16 oz. cream cheese, softened
¾ cup sugar
½ tsp. vanilla extract
12 oz. non-dairy whipped topping, defrosted

Using a hand mixer, blend together first 3 ingredients. Add the non-dairy whipped topping and blend on high speed until fluffy. Pour into pan with the prepared crust. Refrigerate for at least 4 hours.

### BLUEBERRY SAUCE
2 cups fresh or frozen blueberries
½ cup sugar, or a little more to taste
½ cup water
2 tbsp. freshly squeezed lemon juice
2 tbsp. cornstarch
2 tbsp. cold water
½ tsp. vanilla extract

Ethan enjoying his favorite cheesecake!

In a saucepan over medium heat, combine blueberries, sugar, water, and lemon juice. Simmer for 5 minutes. In a small bowl, whisk together 2 tbsp. cornstarch and 2 tbsp. cold water. In a slow, steady stream, add cornstarch mixture to blueberries, stirring constantly to combine. Simmer for 3-5 minutes, or until sauce thickens and coats the back of a metal spoon. Remove from heat and stir in vanilla. Serve cooled with the cheesecake.

Sunday barbecue at Myran's.

# SUNDAY BARBECUE

Eating barbecue on Sundays is a Cajun ritual. My favorite place for Sunday barbecue is Myran's Maison de Manger in Arnaudville, Louisiana. Myran's has been open since 1979. The restaurant is actually housed in the same building where my grandmother Ida used to operate a restaurant back in the 1950s. Myran's barbecue menus usually consist of ribs, chicken, and pork steak. My dad used to cook barbecue most Sundays during my teen years. If he didn't cook, we picked it up from Myran's.

### ~Menu~

Homemade Lemonade
Mulate's Coleslaw
Baked Beans
Rice Dressing
Barbecued Baby Back Ribs
Cajun Barbecued Chicken
Southern Pecan Pie

Arnaudville water tower.

# Homemade Lemonade

*Cool and refreshing, this delicious lemonade goes well with the smoky flavors of barbecue.*

8 cups filtered water, divided
1⅔ cups sugar
1½ cups freshly squeezed lemon juice

In a small pot, make simple syrup by combining sugar and 1 cup water. Bring to a boil and stir until sugar dissolves. Remove from heat and let cool to room temperature, then cover and refrigerate until chilled. Pour the remaining 7 cups of water into a pitcher and stir in the lemon juice. Add the simple syrup and stir until well combined. Refrigerate for at least 1 hour before serving. Makes 8 cups.

# Mulate's Coleslaw

*Coleslaw is the quintessential Cajun side item for Sunday barbecue. When we decided to start serving coleslaw as a side item in the restaurant, I worked on this recipe for weeks. I wanted something special with lots of flavors. This coleslaw also tastes delicious on top of a Barbecued Beef Po' Boy (see Index).*

1 cup mayonnaise
3 tbsp. yellow mustard
¼ cup sliced green onions
¼ cup chopped fresh parsley
2 tbsp. sweet relish
2 tsp. sugar
1½ tsp. black pepper
1½ tsp. garlic powder
9 cups coleslaw cabbage mix

Combine all ingredients except cabbage mix in a large bowl. Mix well. Add cabbage and toss to coat. Serves 8-10.

## Baked Beans

*You could use the beans right out of the can, but this version is so much tastier!*

60 oz. canned pork and beans
½ cup ketchup
½ cup brown sugar
1 tbsp. Worcestershire sauce
1 tbsp. freshly squeezed lemon juice
1 tsp. yellow mustard
1 lb. bacon
1 cup diced onion
¼ cup water

Preheat oven to 375 degrees. In a large bowl, mix together pork and beans, ketchup, brown sugar, Worcestershire sauce, lemon juice, and mustard.

Set aside 6-8 strips of bacon. In a large pan, fry the rest of the bacon until crisp then set aside. Drain off most of the bacon grease, leaving just enough to coat the bottom of the pan. Add onion to the pan and sauté over medium heat. When onion starts to wilt, crumble cooked bacon into the pan and mix well. Add water to deglaze. Cook until onion is transparent. Remove from heat and add onions and bacon to the bean mixture.

Pour into a 9x13 baking pan. Place uncooked strips of bacon on top of beans. Cover with foil and bake for 1 hour. Remove foil, increase heat to 400 degrees, and bake uncovered for 30 minutes. Serves 8-10.

## Rice Dressing

*A must-have for a Cajun Sunday barbecue. You may have heard it called "dirty rice," but in the area of south-central Louisiana known as Acadiana, we call it rice dressing.*

1 tbsp. vegetable oil
1 cup diced onions
1 cup diced bell pepper
3 cloves garlic, minced
1 lb. ground beef
1 lb. ground pork
2 tsp. kosher salt
1½ tsp. red pepper
½ tsp. black pepper
1 tsp. garlic powder
1 cup sliced green onions
3 cups cooked rice

In a large saucepot, heat oil over medium heat. Add onion and bell pepper. Cook for 10 minutes, stirring frequently until onion is transparent. Add garlic and cook for 3 minutes. Add beef and pork, then brown meat for 15 minutes. Add dry seasonings and simmer for 10 minutes. Remove from heat and drain excess grease. Stir in green onions. Fold in rice and mix until well blended. Serves 8.

# Barbecued Baby Back Ribs

*Traditional baby back ribs, done the Cajun way!*

2 racks of pork baby back ribs
2 tbsp. Mulate's Cajun Seasoning
2 tsp. kosher salt
2 cups Jack Miller's Barbecue Sauce
2 tbsp. Steen's Pure Cane Syrup
Charcoal for grilling

Remove the thin membrane from the back of the ribs by slicing into the membrane with a sharp knife and pulling it off the rib meat. Season ribs on both sides with Mulate's Cajun Seasoning and salt. Allow the ribs to sit out at room temperature for about 30 minutes while preparing the grill.

Place the charcoal in your pit and light according to the instructions on the bag. Allow the charcoal to burn down to about 300 degrees. The coals should be covered in ash. Place the ribs on the grill and close the top. Keep the heat between 275-300 degrees by opening and closing the vents on the pit. Cook ribs for 1 hour then turn and cook for another hour. All racks do not cook at the same speed so you will need to check them for doneness. As the meat cooks, it shrinks and exposes the bone at the thinner end of the rib. When about ¼-inch of bone is exposed, the ribs should be done.

Meanwhile, prepare the sauce by combining the barbecue sauce with the cane syrup. After the ribs have cooked for at least 2 hours and you've checked for doneness, baste both sides of the racks with the sauce and cook for 30 minutes more. Pull the racks off the grill, cover them in foil, and let them rest for about 20 minutes before serving. Serves 8.

# Cajun Barbecued Chicken

*Chicken is my barbecued meat of choice, and the thigh is the best part!*

4 chicken halves
2 tbsp. Mulate's Cajun Seasoning
2 tsp. kosher salt
2 cups Jack Miller's Barbecue Sauce
2 tbsp. Steen's Pure Cane Syrup
Charcoal for grilling

Season the chicken halves on both sides with Mulate's Cajun Seasoning and salt. Allow chicken to sit out at room temperature for about 30 minutes while preparing the grill.

Place the charcoal in your pit and light according to the instructions on the bag. Brown both sides of chicken over the hot coals then move them to the side to allow the charcoal to burn down to about 300 degrees. The coals should be covered in ash. Return chicken to the center of the grill and close the top. Keep the heat between 275-300 degrees by opening and closing the vents on the pit. Cook for 30 minutes then rotate the chicken. Cook for another 20 minutes.

Meanwhile, prepare the sauce by combining the barbecue sauce with the cane syrup. Baste the chicken on both sides, then place the chicken with the meat side down and cook for another 10-30 minutes. Since cooking time will vary for each piece of chicken, you will need to test for doneness. In order to do that, insert the tip of a knife into the middle of the thickest piece. If the juices run clear, the chicken is done. Serves 8.

# Southern Pecan Pie

*Must be served warm with a scoop of vanilla ice cream to be truly experienced!*

1 cup white corn syrup
½ cup light brown sugar
3 eggs, whisked
1 tsp. vanilla extract
Pinch of salt
1 cup pecan halves
Pie shell

Preheat oven to 350 degrees. Mix all ingredients together. Pour into pie shell. Bake for 50 minutes.

*Variation:* You can add ¾ cup semisweet morsels for Chocolate Pecan Pie.

Thankful for my family.

# THANKSGIVING DAY

In our family, it's always more about the sides than the turkey. I'm a believer in using full-fat ingredients, especially in these recipes. If there's a time to enjoy rich foods, it's during the holidays. Bring on the real butter!

### ~Menu~

Old Fashioned
Cajun Fried Turkey
Spaghetti & Cheese
Broccoli-Cheese Casserole
Cornbread Dressing
Sweet Potato Crunch
Nana's Shrimp Dressing
Dirt Cake

# Old Fashioned

*The Old Fashioned is a classic cocktail that has seen a recent surge in popularity. When I worked at Mulate's in Baton Rouge, we had a customer who would come in every evening for his nightly cocktail. You knew when he walked in the door to start preparing his drink.*

1 tsp. raw or granulated sugar
3 dashes Angostura bitters
2 oz. rye whiskey
Orange wedge
2 Luxardo maraschino cherries

In an Old Fashioned glass, muddle sugar and bitters with a few drops of water. Add whiskey and stir until sugar is dissolved. Add several large ice cubes and stir to chill. Garnish with a slice of orange and two cherries. Serves 1.

# Cajun Fried Turkey

*Our head chef, Perry Watts, is an expert at making a delicious fried turkey.
We offer it on our private event menu, and our customers are always extremely happy!*

12-15 lb. turkey, rinsed and dried
6 tbsp. Mulate's Cajun Seasoning
3 tsp. kosher salt
Cottonseed oil or peanut oil for frying

Rub Mulate's Cajun Seasoning and salt over the outside of the turkey as well as under the skin of the turkey. In a deep fryer, heat the oil to 250 degrees. Slowly lower the turkey into the fryer. Cook turkey for 3½ minutes per pound. (A 12 lb. turkey would take 40-45 minutes to cook.) Carefully pull the turkey out of the fryer. Allow it to drain before you carve it. Enjoy that crispy skin! Serves 15-20.

***

*Note:* Invest in a good quality outdoor 30-qt. turkey fryer with a "max fill" line, and be sure to read your fryer's manual. It is important that you use enough oil to cover your turkey but not so much that it spills over and creates a fire. A good way to determine how much oil to use is to place the raw turkey in the fryer pot. Fill the pot with water until it covers the turkey, remove the turkey from the pot, and take note of the water level. You will need to fill the pot with oil to the same level.

# Spaghetti & Cheese

*My dad's recipe for this baked spaghetti has always been a staple in my house. The little bit of heat the cayenne pepper adds is my favorite part of this dish.*

Kerry and Monique.

1 lb. spaghetti
1 stick unsalted butter, melted
14 slices American cheese, divided
1 egg, whisked
1 cup whole milk
1 tsp. cayenne pepper

Preheat oven to 350 degrees. Butter a 9x13 baking dish. Boil and drain spaghetti. In a large bowl, mix hot spaghetti, melted butter, and 8 slices of cheese, broken into pieces. When butter and cheese have melted, add egg, milk, and cayenne pepper. Place 6 slices of cheese on top of the spaghetti mixture. Bake for 25-30 minutes. Serves 10.

---

*Note:* You can reduce this recipe by half. However, you should still use 1 egg.

# Broccoli-Cheese Casserole

*This recipe is inspired by the late Sally DeMatteo. Sally's husband, Henry, is Murphy's cousin, and he has worked at Mulate's for more than 20 years. Henry is our jack-of-all-trades, handling everything from deliveries to roof leaks! Sally made this dish one Thanksgiving many years ago, and I changed it a little bit to make it my own.*

4 lb. fresh broccoli florets
2 tbsp. unsalted butter
1 cup diced onions
3 cloves garlic, minced
16 oz. processed cheese, cubed
½ tsp. cayenne pepper
21 oz. canned cream of mushroom soup
16 oz. canned mushrooms
½ cup shredded Cheddar cheese
15 butter crackers, crumbled, for topping

Preheat oven to 350 degrees. Butter a 9x13 baking dish. Blanch broccoli in a pot of boiling water for 5-7 minutes, then drain and transfer to a large mixing bowl. In a medium sauce pot, melt butter over medium heat. Add onions and sauté 3-5 minutes, or until soft. Add garlic and cook for 2 minutes. Add processed cheese and cayenne and stir until melted. Mix in soup and mushrooms, stirring until combined. Pour creamy sauce over broccoli and toss to coat. Pour into prepared baking dish and top with shredded Cheddar and cracker crumbs. Bake for 20-30 minutes, or until cheese is melted and bubbly. Serves 10.

# Cornbread Dressing

*I don't recall a holiday from my childhood when we didn't have this cornbread dressing. This recipe is inspired by my mother's side, the Robin family from Port Barre, Louisiana.*

30 oz. packaged cornbread mix
15 oz. can cream-style corn
32 oz. dressing mix*
1 lb. ground beef
1½-2 qt. whole milk
2 tbsp. butter

Prepare cornbread according to package directions. Mix cream-style corn into batter then bake as directed. Crumble baked cornbread into a large mixing bowl. Set aside.

Preheat oven to 350 degrees. In a large skillet, brown ground beef. Add dressing mix and cook, partially covered, over medium heat, stirring frequently for 10 minutes. Add meat mixture to crumbled cornbread. Mix well, moistening with milk. Pour into 2 separate 9x13 baking pans. Dot the top with butter. Bake for 50 minutes. Serves 10.

---

*Note:* If preparing dressing in advance, cool completely after baking, cover, and refrigerate. When ready to serve, place covered pans in oven at 350 degrees for 30-45 minutes or until heated through.

*Dressing mix is a vegetable, meat, and seasoning mixture. It can be found in the frozen section of your grocer's meat department. If it is unavailable, use 2 lb. ground pork in its place, and sauté 1 diced onion and 1 diced bell pepper in 1 tbsp. vegetable oil before browning the ground meat. You will also need to add 1 tbsp. kosher salt, 2 tsp. black pepper, and 1 tsp. cayenne pepper to the meat mixture.

# Sweet Potato Crunch

*The topping is the best part of this holiday side, which I enjoyed every year as a child. My late father-in-law absolutely loved it as well. It was special to him because it was unlike the sweet potatoes his mother made throughout his life.*

60 oz. canned sweet potatoes, drained or 4 lb. boiled, skinned sweet potatoes
1¼ cups sugar
1 tsp. kosher salt
1 tsp. cinnamon
4 eggs, whisked
1 cup half-and-half or heavy cream
1 tsp. vanilla extract
½ cup unsalted butter, melted

Preheat oven to 350 degrees. Butter a 9x13 baking dish. In a large bowl, mash sweet potatoes then add remaining ingredients. Mix well. Pour into prepared baking dish. (If preparing in advance, cover and refrigerate at this point.) Top with Brown Sugar Topping and bake for 35 minutes. Serves 10-12.

**BROWN SUGAR TOPPING**
16 oz. light brown sugar
⅔ cup flour
⅔ stick butter, melted
2 cups chopped pecans

Combine brown sugar and flour. Add melted butter and chopped pecans. Mix until fully incorporated. Spread on top of sweet potato mixture.

# Nana's Shrimp Dressing

*This recipe is inspired by my husband's grandmother, Mary Grace, whom he called "Nana." She was born in the US to Sicilian parents who settled in New Orleans back in the 1800s. Nana made this dish every Thanksgiving and Christmas. I learned how to make it from her because it's my husband's favorite holiday food, and I have worked for many years to get it to taste as close as possible to hers.*

1 stick unsalted butter
3 cups diced onions
5 cups diced bell pepper
6 cloves garlic, minced
½ cup sliced green onions
½ cup chopped parsley
2 tsp. kosher salt
1 tsp. black pepper
½ tsp. thyme
⅔ cup plain breadcrumbs
8 slices white bread, soaked in 1 cup vegetable broth and squeezed
¼ cup Romano cheese plus extra for topping
½ cup Parmesan cheese plus extra for topping
2 eggs, whisked
2 lb. 40/50 shrimp, peeled and deveined

Monique and Murphy.

Preheat oven to 350 degrees. Butter a 9x13 baking dish. In a large pot, melt butter over medium heat. Add onions and bell pepper. Cook down for 20 minutes or until onions are caramelized. Mix in garlic, green onions, and parsley and cook for 5-7 minutes. Reduce heat to low. Add breadcrumbs, wet bread, cheeses, and eggs, stirring constantly until incorporated. Add shrimp and cook for 3-5 minutes, or until shrimp have just turned pink. Transfer to prepared baking dish and top with Romano and Parmesan cheese. (If preparing in advance, cover and place in the refrigerator at this point.) Bake for 35 minutes. Serves 10.

# Dirt Cake

*This cake is a favorite of my husband's. He loves it so much that we added it to the menu! It's a recipe that was handed down from an important woman in my life, Ms. G, as she was affectionately known to many people. She was awesome in the kitchen and she has inspired my cooking over the years. This is a fairly simple recipe, but it's always a huge hit.*

16 oz. cream cheese
½ cup unsalted butter, melted
½ cup powdered sugar
2⅔ cups cold milk
5 oz. box vanilla instant pudding
12 oz. non-dairy whipped topping
5 cups Oreo cookie crumbs

In large bowl, beat cream cheese, butter, and sugar until smooth. Alternating with the instant pudding, mix in milk until well incorporated. Beat mixture for 2 minutes. Fold in whipped topping and beat until thoroughly combined. In a glass bowl layer Oreo crumbs on the bottom, then alternate between cookie crumbs and filling. Top with a layer of Oreo crumbs. Chill for at least 1 hour before serving. Serves 10-12.

Christmas Eve at home.

# CHRISTMAS EVE

My favorite night of the year! We always had wonderful times at my grandmother Leether's house on Christmas Eve. My mom is from Port Barre, Louisiana. It's a small town about 20 minutes from Arnaudville, where my father was born and raised. Both towns lie in St. Landry Parish, along the banks of Bayou Teche and Bayou Courtableau. We usually have gumbo and other little bites on Christmas Eve, so I like to keep it simple. One of my guests usually picks up a vegetable or fruit tray from the local deli to accompany my Christmas Eve menu.

## ~Menu~

Cosmopolitan
Ida's Crabmeat Mornay
Potato Salad
Zydeco Gumbo
Sand Tarts

# Cosmopolitan

*Even though it may be a little time-consuming, I think these cocktails are best made one at a time.*

The calm before the party.

2 oz. good vodka
1 oz. cranberry juice cocktail
¾ oz. freshly squeezed lime juice
¾ oz. Grand Marnier
Orange twist, for garnish

Combine vodka, cranberry juice, lime juice, and Grand Marnier in a cocktail shaker. Fill shaker with ice, cover, and shake vigorously until outside of shaker is very cold, about 20 seconds. Strain cocktail into a chilled martini glass. Garnish with orange twist. Serves 1.

## Ida's Crabmeat Mornay

*My grandmother's recipe for a delicious, creamy lump crabmeat dip is decadently perfect for the holidays.*

½ stick unsalted butter
1 small bunch green onions, chopped
2 tbsp. flour
1 tsp. salt
1 tsp. cayenne pepper
½ tsp. black pepper
1 cup heavy cream
1 cup half-and-half
2 cups grated Swiss cheese
1 lb. lump crabmeat

In a large pot, melt butter over medium heat. Sauté green onions for 5 minutes. Blend in flour then add salt, cayenne, and black pepper. Add cream, half-and-half, and cheese. Stir constantly until cheese is melted. Fold in crabmeat and continue cooking just long enough for crabmeat to get hot. Serve as a hot dip with Melba toast or in patty shells. Serves 8-10.

## Potato Salad

*Although many people think of potato salad as a cold dish, I like to eat my potato salad at room temperature. I think the flavors come together and taste better when the dish isn't chilled. My maternal grandfather, Roy, taught me to put potato salad in my gumbo instead of rice. Even today, I can't have gumbo without the potato salad!*

4 large potatoes
1 tbsp. Mulate's Cajun Seasoning
1 tsp. kosher salt
4 hard-boiled eggs, halved
¼ cup mayonnaise (or more if you prefer a creamier texture)
1 tbsp. + 1 tsp. yellow mustard
1 tsp. white vinegar
¼ cup sliced green onions
Salt and pepper to taste

Peel potatoes and dice into 1-inch cubes. Boil until tender, then drain. Transfer potatoes to a large mixing bowl, season with Mulate's Cajun Seasoning and salt, and mix well. Separate the egg yolk from the egg white, reserving yolk in a small bowl. Cut whites into the seasoned potato mixture. Mash reserved yolks with the back of a fork and add mayonnaise, mustard, vinegar, and green onions. Mix until smooth. Add seasoned yolks to potato mixture and mix well. Season with salt and pepper to taste. Serves 8-10.

# Zydeco Gumbo

*A customer favorite! Gumbo is always better the day after you make it, so go ahead and make this a day in advance if you're having people over. It's an absolute must-have on Christmas Eve!*

2 lb. boneless, skinless chicken thighs
2 tbsp. Mulate's Cajun Seasoning
1 tbsp. vegetable oil
3 cups diced onions
1 cup diced bell pepper
¼ cup diced celery
5 cloves garlic, minced
30 oz. frozen cut okra
1 tsp. kosher salt
½ tsp. cayenne pepper
4¼ qt. water
1 cup dark roux
1 lb. 50/60 count shrimp, peeled
1 lb. smoked sausage, sliced ¼-inch thick

Season chicken with Mulate's Cajun Seasoning. In a large soup pot, heat oil over medium-high heat. Working in batches so as not to overcrowd the pot, brown the chicken on both sides. Remove chicken from pot and cut into bite-sized pieces. Set aside. Add onion, bell pepper, and celery to the pot and sauté for 5 minutes. Deglaze pot with ½ cup of water. Be sure to scrape all the little browned bits from the sides and bottom of the pot. Add garlic and okra and cook for 20 minutes, adding water as needed to prevent sticking. Season with salt and cayenne and stir until blended. Add 4 qt. water and bring to a boil. Mix in roux and stir until dissolved. Add chicken pieces; return to a boil. Reduce heat and simmer for 40 minutes. Add shrimp and smoked sausage; boil for 10 minutes. Turn off heat and let the gumbo rest for 30-45 minutes before serving over white rice. Serves 8-10.

---

**Note:** You can buy a dark roux (which will save time) in most grocery stores, but you can make your own as well. To make a roux for this recipe, heat 1 cup vegetable oil in a heavy pot or pan. Add 1 cup all-purpose flour and cook over a low heat, stirring constantly until the roux is the color you desire. For this gumbo, the roux should be a chocolate brown color. Making your own roux requires time and patience. You can't rush it!

Zydeco Gumbo with potato salad, my favorite!

# Sand Tarts

*I grew up having these cookies during the Christmas holidays.*

2 sticks unsalted butter, softened
½ cup powdered sugar
½ tsp. vanilla
1¾ cups all-purpose flour, sifted
½ cup finely chopped nuts (I prefer pecans or almonds.)
Powdered sugar for dusting

Preheat oven to 350 degrees. With a hand mixer on medium speed, cream together butter, powdered sugar, and vanilla in a large mixing bowl. Add flour a little at a time, mixing to combine. Add chopped nuts. Shape into small balls, logs, or crescents. Bake on ungreased cookie sheet for 20 minutes. Roll in powdered sugar when cool. Makes 24.

Cajun-Style Frittata & Hash Brown Casserole.

# CHRISTMAS MORNING

I love to cook breakfast for my family of four on Christmas morning. Christmas Day is the only day of the entire year that I devote completely to relaxation. If we venture out, it's usually in the late afternoon or evening. Mulate's is closed on both Christmas Day and Thanksgiving Day in order for our employees to enjoy their time with family and friends.

### ~Menu~

Mimosa
Peanut Butter Chip Banana Muffins
Cajun-Style Frittata
Hash Brown Casserole
Crêpes

## Mimosa

*I love a mimosa before brunch—or really anytime. It's probably my favorite cocktail. I don't use Grand Marnier in mine, but I know some like that extra little kick it provides.*

1 bottle (750 mL) dry sparkling wine or champagne, chilled
3 cups orange juice (freshly squeezed is best), chilled
½ cup Grand Marnier, optional

Hold each champagne flute at a slight angle, and fill halfway with sparkling wine. Fill remainder of glass with orange juice. Top with 1 tbsp. Grand Marnier. Serve promptly. Makes about 8 mimosas.

*Note:* Feel free to adjust the ratio of sparkling wine to orange juice to suit your preference. (I like my mimosas with more sparkling wine than orange juice.)

## Peanut Butter Chip Banana Muffins

*One of my favorite food combinations, peanut butter and banana, makes these muffins irresistible!*

1½ cups all-purpose flour
1 cup sugar
1 tsp. baking soda
3 medium ripe bananas
1 egg, whisked
⅓ cup butter, melted
1 tsp. vanilla extract
½ cup peanut butter chips

Preheat oven to 375 degrees. Line a muffin pan with baking cups. Combine flour, sugar, and baking soda in a large mixing bowl. In a separate mixing bowl, mash the bananas. Add egg, butter, and vanilla. Mix well. Fold in the peanut butter chips. Fill baking cups about half-full. Bake for 20 minutes, or until a toothpick inserted into the center of one of the muffins comes out clean. Makes 12 muffins.

# Cajun-Style Frittata

*My husband's grandmother, Nana, made "Potatoes and Eggs," as she called it. The fancy word is "frittata." I learned how to cook her Potatoes and Eggs because it's one of my husband's favorite things. This is my colorful and lovely Cajun version (without potatoes), perfect for Christmas morning!*

½ cup andouille sausage, cut into ¼-inch wedges
7 eggs, whisked
¼ tsp. kosher salt
¼ tsp. cayenne pepper
1 tbsp. sliced green onions
⅓ cup shredded Cheddar cheese
2 tsp. vegetable or olive oil
¼ cup diced onion
¼ cup diced red bell pepper

Brown andouille in a large non-stick skillet over medium-high heat. Drain andouille on a paper towel and set aside. Wash and dry the skillet to prevent sticking when putting the frittata together. In a large mixing bowl, whisk together eggs, salt, pepper, green onions, and cheese. Mix well to combine and set aside.

In your clean skillet, heat oil over medium heat. Add onion and bell pepper. Sauté for 5 minutes, just until softened. Layer andouille in the skillet. Pour egg mixture evenly over andouille. Allow frittata to begin to set. Using a rubber spatula, move egg mixture around a little bit to be sure it cooks evenly. Run spatula around the edges of the pan. Reduce heat to medium-low. Cook for 10 minutes, using your spatula to check that the egg is not browning too much on the bottom. When the egg is lightly set and the bottom is beginning to brown, place a dinner plate over the top of the frittata. Flip the entire frittata onto the plate. Slide the frittata back into the skillet to cook the top side for about 3-5 minutes. One frittata serves 4-8, depending on how you slice it.

---

*Note:* If you want to double this recipe, double all the ingredients but make a "Cajun Scramble" instead of a frittata. This would be an easier way to make a fabulous egg dish for a crowd.

## Hash Brown Casserole

*Creamy and delicious... This one goes fast in my house!*

2 lb. frozen hash browns, broken into pieces
½ cup unsalted butter, melted
10 oz. can cream of mushroom soup
1 pt. sour cream
½ cup diced onions
2 cups shredded Cheddar cheese
1 tsp. garlic powder
¼ tsp. cayenne pepper

Preheat oven to 350 degrees. Butter an 11x14 casserole dish. Combine all ingredients in a large mixing bowl. Mix well. Pour into prepared dish. (If you are preparing this dish in advance, cover and refrigerate at this point.) Bake for 45-50 minutes. Broil for 2-3 minutes to brown the top. Let stand for 5 minutes before serving. Serves 10-12.

## Crêpes

*My daughter loves to put Nutella and fresh fruit and berries on her crêpes.*

1 cup flour
1 tbsp. sugar
1 tsp. kosher salt
1½ cups milk
2 eggs, whisked
½ tsp. butter

In a mixing bowl, combine flour, sugar, and salt. Add milk and eggs and mix well to combine. In a large skillet, melt butter over medium-high heat, but do not brown. Add ½ cup of batter and tilt skillet in a circular motion to create a thin crêpe. Once the crêpe is brown on the underside, flip and cook 1 minute more. Makes 5-6 crêpes.

Maia's Nutella Crêpe.

Make learning to Cajun dance your New Year's resolution!

# NEW YEAR'S DAY

According to Southern tradition, you will have good luck throughout the year if you eat the traditional New Year's Day meal. Black-eyed peas symbolize coins or wealth. The pork flavoring the beans is considered a sign of prosperity. Greens like cabbage symbolize money, and cornbread symbolizes gold. It was only when I started dating my husband, who is originally from New Orleans, that I learned about the traditional New Year's Day foods. Now I cook this special meal every single year because it's fun. One year, we were traveling on New Year's Day, so I made all the dishes the following week once we returned home!

### ~Menu~

Bourbon Milk Punch
Shredded Cabbage Salad
Smothered Cabbage
Black-Eyed Peas
Cornbread
Cajun Fig Cake

# Bourbon Milk Punch

*My husband's daytime drink of choice!*

Here's to the New Year!

2 cups low-fat milk
⅔ cup half-and-half
1 tbsp. vanilla extract
1¼ cups good bourbon (I prefer Woodford Reserve.)
⅓ cup powdered sugar
Freshly ground nutmeg for garnish

In a pitcher, combine milk, half-and-half, vanilla, and bourbon. Add powdered sugar and stir until blended. Pour over ice into individual glasses and top with ground nutmeg. Makes 4 drinks.

# Shredded Cabbage Salad

*My friend, who helped with a few details of this cookbook, told me that her family always serves both cooked and raw cabbage on New Year's Day since not everyone likes their cabbage cooked.*

8 cups shredded cabbage
¼ cup apple cider vinegar
1 tbsp. sugar
1 tsp. black pepper
½ tsp. salt
¼ cup sliced green onions
Sliced almonds, optional
Cranberries, optional
½ cup diced apples, optional

Place shredded cabbage in a large, chilled bowl. In a small mixing bowl, combine apple cider vinegar, sugar, pepper, salt, and green onions. Add to the cabbage and toss to coat. Fold in your choice of optional toppings. Serves 12-15.

# Smothered Cabbage

*This is a basic, easy recipe for smothered cabbage. And it's vegetarian. If you would like to make the dish a little heartier, add 2 links of diced smoked sausage after you sauté the onions.*

1 tbsp. extra virgin olive oil
1 cup diced onions
3 cloves garlic, minced
1 head cabbage, quartered and sliced
1 cup vegetable stock
2 tsp. kosher salt
1 tsp. black pepper
1 tsp. red pepper flakes

In a large pot, heat oil over medium heat. Sauté onion for 5 minutes. Add garlic and cook for 2 minutes. Add vegetable stock and stir to deglaze the pan. Reduce heat to low, add cabbage, and cook, covered, for 15-20 minutes, or until cabbage is tender. Stir occasionally and add water as needed to prevent sticking. Stir in salt, black pepper, and red pepper flakes. Remove from heat. Serves 6-8.

# Black-Eyed Peas

*I like to spice up this dish with a few dashes of our Mulate's Cayenne Pepper Sauce!*

- 2 cups diced onions
- 1 cup diced bell pepper
- ¼ cup diced celery
- 1 lb. pickled pork
- 2 cloves garlic, minced
- 1½ tbsp. Mulate's Cajun Seasoning
- 2 tsp. salt
- 1 lb. black-eyed peas, rinsed and drained
- 6 cups water
- 4 cups reduced sodium chicken broth

In a large pot over medium heat, sauté onion, bell pepper, and celery for 15 minutes. Meanwhile, in a separate pot, boil the pickled pork for 10 minutes to remove excess salt. Drain and set aside. Add garlic to the sautéed vegetables and cook for 3 minutes. Stir in Mulate's Cajun Seasoning and salt. Add pickled pork, peas, water, and broth. Cover and simmer on low for 2½-3 hours, stirring occasionally, until beans are soft. Uncover and cook for 15 minutes. Serve over rice. Serves 8.

*Note:* This recipe is easily doubled, but you should use 3 cups of diced onion and 1½ cups of diced bell pepper.

# Cornbread

*I like sweet cornbread with real butter on top, but if you'd prefer a little less sugar, use ½ cup instead.*

1 cup cornmeal
2⅓ cups all-purpose flour
1½ tbsp. baking powder
1 tsp. salt
1½ sticks unsalted butter, softened
1 cup sugar
3 eggs, whisked
1⅔ cups whole milk

Preheat oven to 400 degrees. In a large bowl, combine cornmeal, flour, baking powder, and salt; mix well. In a separate large bowl, using a hand mixer, cream together butter and sugar until light and fluffy. Add eggs and mix well. Alternating, add ½ cup of milk and ½ cup of the dry ingredient mixture, mixing until all is blended. Pour into a greased 9x13 pan. Bake for 25 minutes or until a toothpick inserted in the middle comes out clean.

# Cajun Fig Cake

*I make this cake a few times a year for my dad. It's one of his favorite sweets.*

- 2 cups all-purpose flour, sifted
- 2 tsp. cinnamon
- 1 tsp. salt
- 1 tsp. baking soda
- ½ cup sugar
- 3 eggs
- ⅔ cup oil
- 8 oz. sour cream
- 1½-2 cups fig preserves with syrup
- 1 cup chopped pecans

Preheat oven to 350 degrees. Prepare a 9x13 baking pan with non-stick spray. In a mixing bowl, combine flour, cinnamon, salt, and baking soda and set aside. In a separate mixing bowl, using a hand mixer, combine sugar and eggs. Blend in oil and sour cream. Add dry mixture to wet mixture. Stir in figs and pecans. Pour into prepared pan and bake for 40-45 minutes, or until a toothpick inserted in cake comes out clean.

# INDEX

Arugula Salad ............................................. 115
Baked Beans .............................................. 124
Baked Spirals and Cheese ......................... 67
Bananas Foster .......................................... 70
Barbecued Baby Back Ribs ....................... 125
Barbecued Beef Po' Boy ............................ 52
Black-Eyed Peas ........................................ 154
Blackened Shrimp au Gratin ..................... 41
Blueberry Cobbler ..................................... 70
Boiled Crawfish .......................................... 93
Bourbon Milk Punch ................................. 152
Braised Short Ribs ..................................... 117
Broccoli Cheese Casserole ....................... 133
Butter Rum Sauce ..................................... 97
Cajun Barbecued Chicken ......................... 126
Cajun Cobb Salad ...................................... 25
Cajun Fig Cake ........................................... 157
Cajun Fried Turkey .................................... 131
Cajun Frittata ............................................. 147
Cajun Smothered Chicken ........................ 55
Cajun-Style Party Mix ................................ 108
Catfish Jambalaya ...................................... 30
Catfish Mulate's ......................................... 31
Champagne Punch .................................... 84
Chicken & Sausage Gumbo ...................... 22
Chili ............................................................. 110
Chocolate Pecan Fudge Icing ................... 111
Chocolate Sheet Cake ............................... 111

Corn Macque Choux .................................. 104
Cornbread .................................................. 156
Cornbread Dressing .................................. 132
Cosmopolitan ............................................ 140
Crab Cakes with Spicy Cajun Aioli ............ 32
Crabmeat au Gratin ................................... 35
Crawfish Bisque ......................................... 20
Crawfish Bread .......................................... 38
Crawfish Cream Sauce .............................. 37
Crawfish Étouffée ...................................... 39
Crawfish Fettuccine ................................... 39
Crawfish Pie ............................................... 40
Creamed Spinach ...................................... 118
Creamy Oyster Pasta ................................. 47
Crêpes ........................................................ 148
Deviled Eggs .............................................. 86
Dirt Cake .................................................... 137
Easy Lasagna ............................................. 58
Fluffy Cheesecake with Blueberry Sauce .. 119
French Muffaletta ...................................... 109
Fried Oyster Caesar Salad ........................ 27
Frog Leg Sauce Piquante .......................... 59
Garlic Bread ............................................... 118
Hash Brown Casserole .............................. 148
Herb-Roasted Broccoli .............................. 65
Homemade Lemonade ............................. 123
Hot Buffalo Chicken Dip ........................... 110
How to Stock a Bar .................................... 80

| | |
|---|---|
| Ida's Crabmeat Mornay | 141 |
| Lemon Icebox Pie | 71 |
| Mimosa | 146 |
| Mini Po' Boys | 95 |
| Mint Iced Sweet Tea | 100 |
| Mulate's Chicken & Sausage Jambalaya | 96 |
| Mulate's Coleslaw | 123 |
| Mulate's Crabmeat Stuffing | 34 |
| Mulate's Homemade Bread Pudding | 97 |
| Mulate's Special Soft-Shell Crab | 37 |
| Nana's Shrimp Dressing | 136 |
| New Orleans-Style Barbecued Shrimp | 46 |
| Old Fashioned | 130 |
| Painkiller | 108 |
| Panéed Chicken Breast | 56 |
| Party Planning Guide | 78 |
| Peanut Butter Chip Banana Muffins | 146 |
| Pecan Mini Muffin | 87 |
| Pesto Pasta with Sautéed Shrimp | 44 |
| Pesto Sauce | 44 |
| Pineapple-Coconut Bread Pudding | 72 |
| Pork Roast | 53 |
| Potato Salad | 141 |
| Pralines | 73 |
| Quick Cheese Grits | 88 |
| Red Beans & Rice | 54 |
| Red Sangria | 115 |
| Rice Dressing | 124 |
| Rich & Creamy Cheesecake | 73 |
| Roast | 50 |
| Roast Beef Debris Po' Boy | 51 |
| Roasted Asparagus | 62 |
| Roasted Brussels Sprouts | 62 |
| Roasted Cauliflower & Broccoli with Pesto Sauce | 64 |
| Roasted Corn & Shrimp Bisque | 23 |
| Sand Tarts | 143 |
| Sautéed Haricots Verts | 67 |
| Shredded Cabbage Salad | 153 |
| Shrimp & Grits | 88 |
| Shrimp Étouffée | 43 |
| Shrimp Remoulade | 26 |
| Sliced Tomatoes & Mayonnaise | 100 |
| Smothered Cabbage | 153 |
| Smothered Okra with Shrimp | 41 |
| Smothered Seven Steaks ("Rice 'n Gravy") | 103 |
| Sock It to Me Cake | 105 |
| Southern Pecan Pie | 127 |
| Spaghetti & Cheese | 132 |
| Spicy Blue Cheese Dressing | 25 |
| Spicy Cajun Aioli | 32 |
| Spicy New Potato Mash | 66 |
| Spicy Smoked Tuna Dip | 87 |
| Spinach & Artichoke Dip | 95 |
| Stuffed Mushrooms | 34 |
| Stuffed Potatoes | 66 |
| Sweet Potato Crunch | 135 |
| Tarragon-Roasted Cauliflower | 65 |
| Tropical Rum Sauce | 72 |
| Unstuffed Cabbage Rolls | 57 |
| White Sangria | 92 |
| Yogurt Parfait | 89 |
| Zydeco Gumbo | 142 |

# INDEX

Can Double

| | |
|---|---|
| Arugula Salad | 115 |
| Baked Beans | 124 |
| Barbecued Baby Back Ribs | 125 |
| Black-Eyed Peas | 154 |
| Bourbon Milk Punch | 152 |
| Braised Short Ribs | 117 |
| Cajun Barbecued Chicken | 126 |
| Cajun-Style Party Mix | 108 |
| Champagne Punch | 84 |
| Chili | 110 |
| Corn Macque Choux | 104 |
| Creamed Spinach | 118 |
| Deviled Eggs | 86 |
| French Muffaletta | 109 |
| Garlic Bread | 118 |
| Hash Brown Casserole | 148 |
| Homemade Lemonade | 123 |
| Hot Buffalo Chicken Dip | 110 |
| Mini Po' Boys | 95 |
| Mint Iced Sweet Tea | 100 |
| Mulate's Chicken & Sausage Jambalaya | 96 |
| Mulate's Coleslaw | 123 |
| Mulate's Homemade Bread Pudding | 96 |
| Painkiller | 108 |
| Peanut Butter Chip Banana Muffins | 146 |
| Pecan Mini Muffins | 87 |
| Potato Salad | 141 |
| Quick Cheese Grits | 88 |
| Red Sangria | 115 |
| Rice Dressing | 124 |
| Sand Tart | 143 |
| Shredded Cabbage Salad | 153 |
| Shrimp & Grits | 88 |
| Sliced Tomatoes & Mayonnaise | 101 |
| Smothered Cabbage | 153 |
| Smothered Seven Steaks "Rice 'n Gravy" | 103 |
| Spicy Smoked Tuna Dip | 87 |
| Spinach & Artichoke Dip | 95 |
| White Sangria | 92 |
| Yogurt Parfait | 89 |
| Zydeco Gumbo | 142 |